Front and back covers. Sakonnet Point Mural.
Courtesy of Pam Carter. © Art Students League of New York.

This fanciful mural, c.1930, by Reginald Marsh (1899-1954), is painted on the brick facing above the living room fireplace in the stucco house with two chimneys, shown on the left of the back cover—then the Marsh family house, later Osborn, later Morton, now Carter.

The mural incorporates different eras. Its right half (front cover) shows the *Islander*, which went out of service in 1917. Along the top are the ferry landing, dance hall and more, and on the left half (back cover), the imposing Lyman House—all remembered in this book.

Below the Lyman House is Shaw's Wharf, later the site of the Sakonnet Yacht Club; below it the Marsh house; and below that the pier on the rocks in front of the Getchell house (not visible). The four women on the pier are almost certainly the four Getchell sisters: Genie (later Hart, then Rawson), Celie (French), Joan (Cole) and Martha (Harrall). That pier, like all the buildings along the top of the mural, was wiped out in '38.

Published in the United States by Little Compton Historical Society.

ISBN 978-0-9827069-1-6

Library of Congress Catalog Card Number: 2011930012

First Printing: May 2011

Printed in the United States of America by Sheridan Books, Inc.

Designed by Tom Callahan.

Oil painting by A.E. Covell. 1892. Private Collection.

Sakonnet Point Perspectives

Written by James C. Garman and Michelle G. Styger

A collaborative effort of

Friends of the Sakonnet Lighthouse

Little Compton Historical Society

Sakonnet Preservation Association

Oral and Written Histories

Table of Contents

From the Authors

This book is intended to provide an overview of human activity at Sakonnet Point from the distant past to very recent times. The project sponsors, the Little Compton Historical Society (LCHS), the Sakonnet Preservation Association, and the Friends of the Sakonnet Lighthouse undertook an extensive program of oral history from people who remember the Point in its heyday, or at the very least, in the aftermath of its heyday. These stories have been crucial to understanding the Point. We have been gratified and overwhelmed by the richness of the stories derived from the oral histories.

Definitions of what constitutes Sakonnet Point are perhaps as numerous as ways to spell the word "Sakonnet." A 1954 manuscript in the LCHS lists as many as 41 different spellings. For the purpose of this project, Sakonnet Point is defined as the area running from the Stone House south and west, encompassing the breakwater and harbor, Lloyd's Beach, the Sakonnet Point Lighthouse, East and West Islands, and the area between Round and Long Ponds.

Although we have tried to be as comprehensive as possible, the size and scope of this project did not allow for every topic to be explored to its fullest. We hope we have done some justice to the complexities of the past at Sakonnet and that this volume will serve as a starting point, rather than a conclusion, to further interpretations of the Point's complex heritage.

We are extraordinarily grateful to Marjory O'Toole and Fred Bridge of the Little Compton Historical Society for their help with the project. Marjory was a terrific editor, and made this volume much more readable than it would have been otherwise. Fred patiently pulled together the Historical Society's vast resources on Sakonnet Point. We would also like to thank James E. Garman of Portsmouth, who shared his wealth of information on Sakonnet Point with us, especially on the steamboats.

Thanks to everyone who made the project a success. It's been a pleasure for us to investigate this delightful corner of the world, and to learn about its millennia of history.

James C. Garman
Michelle G. Styger

From the Collaborators

For over a year Friends of the Sakonnet Lighthouse, Little Compton Historical Society and Sakonnet Preservation Association have been working together to create *Sakonnet Point Perspectives*. This project is our first collaboration and we couldn't be happier with the results.

Our goal was to document the importance of Sakonnet Point from a variety of perspectives: historical, environmental, economic and cultural. Our greatest resource in this endeavor has been the recollections of people who are connected to the Point. Their oral and written histories, over 40 of them, are woven into this book and bring the Point to life. We are so grateful to them and to their interviewers for sharing their perspectives with us.

We are also most grateful to:

- our funders, the Rhode Island Council for the Humanities and The Newport County Fund of The Rhode Island Foundation,
- our authors, Dr. James C. Garman and Michelle Styger for their months of diligent research and writing,
- our designer, Tom Callahan, who worked magic, and
- our project manager, 'borrowed' from LCHS, Marjory O'Toole.

Finally, as three volunteer-driven organizations, we thank the dozens of volunteers who donated thousands of hours to this project. The Project Committee Members: Shelley Bowen, Fred Bridge, Abigail Brooks, Randy Byers, Kerrin Callahan, Sandy and Piper Hawes, Lease Plimpton, Mike Steers, and Bob Wolter; the Exhibit Preview Party Committee, the Family Day Committee, our editors, advisors, image selectors, donors/lenders of images and objects, and exhibition installers.

We hope you enjoy *Sakonnet Point Perspectives* and will join all three of our organizations in preserving this community we love.

Mike Steers
Friends of the Sakonnet Lighthouse

Robert Wolter
Little Compton Historical Society

Abigail Brooks
Sakonnet Preservation Association

Sakonnet Road. Photograph. c. 1918. Courtesy of the Kelley Family.

Introduction

Now, the road lost itself between thick hedges of wild-rose and elder bloom and now opened up broad views of the dark blue ocean that made the heart leap with their sudden splendor.

Poet Sarah Helen Whitman on the journey to Sakonnet, 1869

The splendor of Sakonnet Point still has the power to make hearts leap, but the Point we see today only hints at the places it once was.

Sakonnet Point offers today's visitors glimpses of the past; a stray wood-shingled building, a cement slab with no apparent purpose, the remnants of an ancient dock extending into the harbor. Past residents would recognize only pieces of what was once their Sakonnet Point. Were they alive today, Awashonks and Benjamin Church might recognize parts of Sakonnet's shoreline; Colonel Henry T. Sisson would see his familiar 19th century Stone House; and turn-of-the-century day trippers would remember the approach to the harbor and its quaint landing place. But the passage of time, changing notions of leisure in America, and the fury of three twentieth-century hurricanes have erased much of the past.

Today the power of the natural landscape prevails over the memories of the past at Sakonnet Point. A walk through the stone pillars of Lloyd's

Beach rewards visitors with one of the most stunning views on the New England coast. The natural beauty of the place makes it difficult to imagine the hustle of activity that characterized the Point a century ago: the steamer *Queen City* loading potatoes for its daily run to Providence, servants at the Lyman House readying rooms for the arrival of visitors, or fishermen emerging from their cabins to begin a new day along the scup lines crossing the mouth of the Sakonnet River.

More recent memories of Sakonnet Point are still vivid; memories of fishing boats returning with 400 pound swordfish, of children learning to swim from the dock of the Sakonnet Yacht Club, and of vanished places like Marcus Wilcox' Fish Market, the Cove Market and the Fo'c's'le. But to trace the history of the Point, we need to start much farther in the past to nearly 8,000 years ago, when the first Native Americans found their way to Sakonnet, 'the place where the water pours forth.'

Sakonnet Harbor. Photograph. c. 1880. LCHS Collection.

Native Americans at Sakonnet

Four thousand years ago Sakonnet's Native Americans might easily have walked between Newport and Sakonnet, crossing a shallow, muddy channel that would eventually become the Sakonnet River. In many ways, the nature of Native American settlement at Sakonnet Point over the last 10,000 years is a mystery. Numerous stone tools, including net sinkers and projectile points, have been found but no systematic archaeological survey has ever been undertaken.

Until approximately 3,500 years ago, when sea levels stabilized, the Point would have been an upland environment, with only a small brackish channel running to its west. In this landscape, East and West Islands would have been high hills, rather than islands. With the rising of the Sakonnet River, many early archaeological sites were flooded and now lie under water, inaccessible to archaeologists.

Despite the absence of documented sites, the memory of Native Americans at Sakonnet Point has survived to this day.

> *I'm sure that the Indians loved Sakonnet Point in the summertime. Absolutely loved it. And there's no question that they fished heavily there, because I've got all these fishnet sinkers I found out on the southern tip of Sakonnet Point... They didn't really live there, they camped there. That was the nature of their lives.*
>
> *Nate Atwater, Oral History, 2010*

For generations, Little Compton's Sakonnet Indians left their winter home in the area now known as Wilbours Woods and spent each summer at Sakonnet Point. There they lived off the bounty of the sea. Roger Williams noted that Native Americans throughout New England tended to live in winter hunting camps in the interior, moving to traditional seaside encampments in the summer.

The Point's location, more or less half-way between the cliffs at Gay Head (Aquinnah) and Aquidneck Island, made it an important topographical point to the area's Native Americans. *The Legend of Sakonnet Rock,* gathered by William Simmons, indicates a significance that may have been more than just geographic.

> *The Giant Moshup, who made Martha's Vineyard, Nantucket, and Cuttyhunk, changed his many children into killer whales when white settlers started to crowd his territory. He quickly tired of his wife Squant's mourning for their children and threw her to Sakonnet. There she demanded contributions from everyone who passed by water. Eventually Squant grew so cruel, the Great Spirit turned her to stone and the English quarried away her arms and head in fear of her.*

Squant's rocky remains are still visible on Lloyd's Beach today.

The *Diary of King Philip's War* is one of the first written records providing us with an account of Sakonnet Point. It vividly retells Benjamin Church's encounter with the Sakonnets at Lloyd's Beach during the war. Torn between the demands of the English and King Philip, Awashonks moved her people from Sakonnet to take shelter with the Narragansetts. They suffered terribly during The Great Swamp Fight and spent a desperate winter with other refugees on Wachusett Mountain. In the spring of 1676, Awashonks led her starving people home to Sakonnet and the promise of food at their seaside camp.

Benjamin Church, was canoeing along the Point in an effort to rejoin his wife and children on Aquidneck Island, when he spied several members of Awashonks' tribe fishing from the shoreline. Years later Church provided this account of the encounter, told in his third-person voice:

> *The enemy hallooed and made signs for the canoe to come ashore. But when they approached them, they skulked and hid in the clefts of the rocks. Then Mr. Church ordered the canoe to be paddled off again, lest if he came too near they should fire upon him.*[1]

Church eventually convinced the men to meet him on the beach at the very end of the Point, "a place where a man might see who was near him." Church was able to give one of the Sakonnets, 'Honest George,' a message to pass on to Awashonks. Their subsequent meeting farther north at Treaty Rock sealed an alliance that placed the Sakonnets under the protection of the English and enlisted Awashonks' warriors in Church's Indian Company. Their alliance was an important step in strengthening Church's position, ultimately leading to the capture and death of King Philip, the end of the war and the opening of Little Compton and New England to further European settlement.

Awashonks at Treaty Rock. Oil Painting by Dora Atwater Millikin. 2010. LCHS Collection.

Awashonks and her step-son, Mamanuah, vied with each other for control of Sakonnet land prior to and after King Philip's War. Awashonks found herself without a home and was granted a small area of land for her band of Sakonnets as a reward for her service to the English. Mamanuah continued to sell land to the Plimouth Proprietors until the end of the 17th century. He saved the lots by the sea for last.

Little Compton-Sakonnet Point Connection

Carlton Brownell – Of course the Point always had a great attraction for teenagers, you know. Our parents never liked us going down there. We'd say we're going to the Point on bicycles or something. "Why do you want to hang out down there?" my father would say. Well that was just the reason we wanted to hang out around there. There were a lot of late teenagers, I mean they were older than we were. And to us they were pretty adventurous and dangerous. Now looking back they were a little questionable. But you know they were sophisticated, we thought.

John Goulart – No. No. We really didn't have any reason to go to the Point. I didn't fish then when I was young, so no reason to go to the Point. Furthest we would probably go is to Brownell Rose Gardens because we used to go down to the beach for seaweed. Other than that, it was just too far to go all the way to Sakonnet Point.

The only time I remember Sakonnet Point is when we had a drought. My dad used to go with the horse and team with barrels to get water out of Round Pond. I think a lot of people did, too. Forget what year there was a drought. We didn't have the wells we have today, and our pond went dry. So we'd go down there to get water for the cows.

Virginia Watt – I had two brothers Richard and Francis Bullock. They were fishermen and they were always at Sakonnet Point but we didn't have a car and we never went to Sakonnet. We lived on Willow Avenue. They had a car. My brother Richard, "Dick" they called him, the oldest one, he was the one that powered the boat that went to West Island when the fireman had to go over there. He took them over in the boat when the hotel that was there burned up. My brother Dick fished all the time and he had what they call fruit boats that went from Sakonnet down south and back. I do remember going down there when there was a bowling alley. I remember doing that a couple of times. See my mother didn't have a car so we weren't down there that much but we ate a lot of fish.

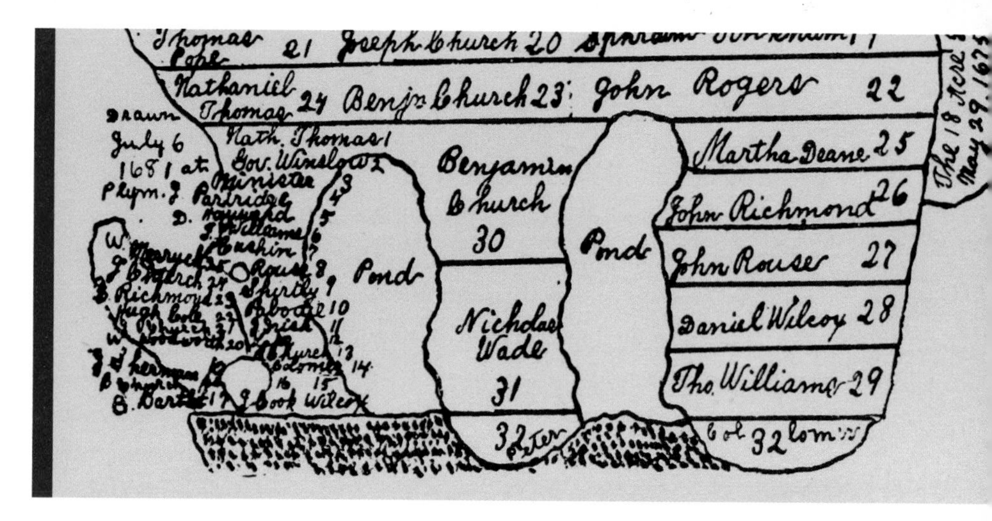

The Plymouth Proprietor's drew lots for Sakonnet Point on July 6, 1681. Approximately 16 English families originally owned a piece of its shoreline including Churches, Irishes, Richmonds, Pabodies, the local minister and Governor Winslow of Plymouth Colony.

Early EuroAmericans at Sakonnet Point

Sakonnet Point was very thinly settled by EuroAmericans until the 19th century. The landscape was dominated by a single large farm owned or occupied by a series of historically significant families. Curiously, Benjamin Church is listed as the First Proprietor of Lot 30, a piece of land located between Long and Round Ponds now called Gardiner's Bluff. Benjamin's brother Joseph soon became the owner of this lot which eventually became the heart of a thriving family enterprise known as Seaconnet Farm. Around the time of the Revolutionary War, Joseph's great-grandson, Colonel Thomas Church added a windmill to the farm.

Little Compton historian, Carlton Brownell agrees that this location is the site of the earliest European presence at Sakonnet Point. "The farm here was called, in various deeds and wills, the Neck Farm, Point Farm, and Sakonnet Farm," he writes, "The oldest house at the Point, demolished in the 19th century…may have been the house owned by the Churches and was probably the scene of the Taggart murder."[2]

The Taggart murder on Seaconnet Farm was Little Compton's single deadly encounter during the Revolutionary War. In her recent book, *The History of Little Compton, First Light: Sakonnet,* Janet Lisle has provided a compelling narrative of this ugly incident.[3] During the Revolution, Little Compton seized the Church Farm from its new owner, a Tory, Gideon Sisson and gave it to the Taggart family as a reward for their patriotism. Judge William Taggart and his family had passed intelligence to the American army and were now refugees from the British-occupied town of Middletown. Having burned the Taggart's home on Aquidneck Island, the British sent a detachment of Loyalist troops to Little Compton to pursue them. The soldiers landed at Sakonnet Point and captured two guards and the two Taggart brothers. Years later the surviving brother wrote that his brother "attempted to escape by leaping over a stone wall, where he was fired on and wounded in the thigh. One of the merciless desperadoes pursued and ran him through with a bayonet."[4]

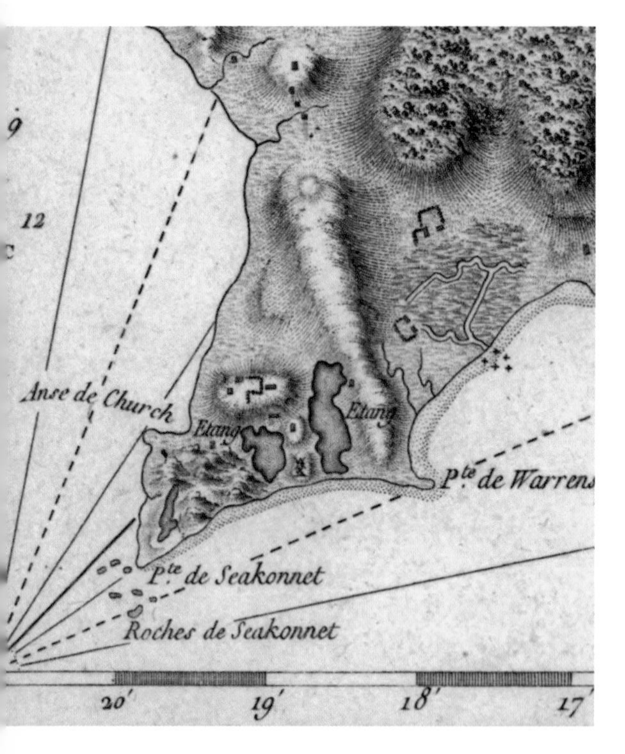

The Church Farm as it appears on Britain's Blaskowitz map, 1777. Note the windmill and farmhouse on the hills.
Courtesy of The Library of Congress.

After the war, the house and the surrounding property were acquired by Patrick Jeffrey, a merchant of Boston, as a speculative venture. In July 1793 he sold the parcel, comprising 242 ¾ acres and a dwelling house, stable, grist mill, outhouses, yards, gardens, and meadows to William Rotch (also spelled "Roach" and "Roache") a Quaker merchant of Nantucket and New Bedford.[5] Jeffrey was a business associate of Rotch and may have purchased the farm at his direction. Rotch would continue to hold the property for nearly three decades, although he may not have actually lived there.

Whether or not Rotch was a resident of Little Compton, he did prove to be a benefactor to the Town. An agreement between Rotch and the Town dating from 1796 notes that the Town had recently opened "a highway of Five rods wide from the Main Road Leading into the Neck and continuing as far as the North side of the Point Farm belonging to sd William Rotch."[6] With no money specified in the agreement, Rotch granted the Town and its residents "a priviledge at the Fishing place Cove…[and] to Cart up Seaweed, and leave the same on the Beach to be carted away when most convenient."[7] Rotch also allowed the Town to build wharves along the Cove, and to land boats along the beach, "and to keep them there at their own pleasure."[8] On one point, however, Rotch was most adamant: "No Priviledge is granted for any House, Store or other building to be erected on the premises," a foreshadowing of centuries of property issues on the Point.

The Mill on Gardiner's Bluff. Early glass plate negative. c. 1870. LCHS Collection.

What happened to the Church-Rotch house is not at all clear. On migrating to Little Compton from Portsmouth, the Lemuel Sisson family took up residence there as Rotch's tenants.[9]

The last appearance of the Church-Rotch House is in a photograph in the LCHS. Taken circa 1870, the photograph shows a windmill, the grist mill mentioned in the deed above, perched on the southern of the two knolls. At the center stands the Church-Rotch house, a sprawling post-medieval house with a steeply-pitched gable and a surprisingly diminutive chimney. Finally, behind the house is a small, vertical-sided English barn very similar in size and configuration to the one presently used by the Little Compton Historical Society for its archives. The house may have been demolished sometime after the Civil War or it may simply have gradually disappeared from the landscape.

Although a fishing presence was established early, few EuroAmericans came to settle at Sakonnet permanently until the third decade of the nineteenth century. Curiously, both East and West Islands, perhaps the least hospitable places in the vicinity, had houses by the time of the Great Gale of 1815. Several sources indicate that fishermen Jeremy Bailey and Andrew Seabury were living on East and West Islands, respectively. These men eked out solitary existences on the desolate rocks, at the very edge of the world. Only with the arrival of the Sisson family as tenants of William Rotch and the beginnings of the fishing industry in the 1830s would there be anyone else at Sakonnet Point.

Sakonnet Harbor. Postcard. c. 1910. Courtesy of James E. Garman.

Fishing

Fred Torphy – Life centered around fishing—fishing and crabbing and minnowing. It had a magic to it and it still has a hold on me. That's why I go down and see what's happening with the few people that are left who do the winter fishing. There is always something interesting going on there, whether it be different kinds of fish that are coming in, or the weather. It's always different but it's magnetic for me.

Susan Cory – My Grandfather and Uncle Wilcox always let kids go out on the *Nasuluga* with them. Some of the kids were six, seven years old. Grandchildren younger than that. My mother loved to go out on the boat. We lived in East Providence so we would get up about 4:30 in the morning because we knew that the boat left the dock at 7:00 and it didn't wait. We were city kids so I think they used to try to make us sea sick. They thought that was fun. So when you are tied up to the trap, the boat would be rolling back and forth and it wasn't too hard to get seasick, between that and the exhaust from the diesel. And Ross Simmons chewing tobacco and talking about runny, gooey eggs. All kinds of things that they could think of just to make us squirm and turn a little green. It was wonderful. We loved it. Our only job was to stay out of the way of the men. Don't interfere.

John Goulart – The sport fishermen were only a handful. Carl Haffenreffer was one of them. Birdie Nightingale—he had the *Good Tern*. Lanny Parker was one of them and Bud Phillips. Cang Lloyd. We were the ones that went out almost every morning. Noel Field. He was a lawyer and he fished with his wife. The name of his boat was *Piscicide*. Those are about the four I know of that went out of Sakonnet in the morning. Dr. Bundy used to go out sometimes, but he wasn't one of the regulars. We had the best boat [*The Juanita*]. Carl Haffenreffer had his boat built also. He and Carol, it's a funny thing, they would come out in the morning, and we all had phones, so I'd be fishing, maybe near Newport, and they never went that far. I used to fish a lot in the Sheep Pen. I'd be out there earlier than they would, and then I'd get a call. And then we'd rendezvous at Carl Haffenreffer's boat for coffee. Yeah, I had a phone on my boat. Usually there was Birdie Nightingale, Noel Field, and Carl Haffenreffer and myself that would join at his boat for coffee.

Phil Marvell – I used to work on the fishing boats. I used to go sword-fishing a lot and I worked the nets with Carl Wilcox and the whole gang on the *Nasuluga*. You know it was filthy dirty work. I used to get the dirty jobs. Like when they pulled nets out, they always had me under the net, the dirty net, and everything just falling on top of me. And I always had to pick out the dirty fish and so I smelled so bad, but it was amazing. It was the best summer I ever had, smelling bad.

Bill Mackintosh – Tony Parascandolo has run the H.N. Wilcox Fish Trap Company since 1968 with the help of his two sons Anthony and Allen. The local lobstermen depend on the trap company to catch their lobster bait and the local gillnet fleet sell their catch to the Parascandolo fish company.

George Mendonsa – I was a commercial fisherman in this area and my father started trap fishing in 1910 when he came from the old country. After the war my brothers and I, we went fishing in the Newport area. So I guess we fished here for, I don't know close to 50, 60 years. Of course we were familiar with the Manchesters and the Wilcoxes. So a couple years ago, well my brothers all died on me and fishing regulations got tough. And I thought, 'Well, the hell with it. Might as well sell everything.' So Alan Wheeler down there he bought half of our fishing operation. And the other half of it another fellow bought. So Wheeler, Alan, asked me if I'd go down there fishing so they could get used to our operation. So I was down there for a couple of years.

Andrea Phillips – Bud was the epitome of the Captain. I would do all the work and he would sit on the bridge and drink coffee and come down for an occasional photo with a big fish. And yet I married him. He had many good traits and he was a funny, funny man. He was just a charming man. When the kids were little, we were always at the Point. For one thing, when you're on a sport boat the rails are fairly high. It's almost like they're in a playpen. They can't get over unless they really climb. And they certainly always had to wear life jackets. We would go out tautog fishing and that kind of stuff when they were little. We always had their birthday parties on the boat; an array of kids. That was always fun. Both Weatherly and Cap at some point would crew for Bud once I got out of it. You know it was a wonderful way of life—to see the fish, meet the people and be out on the ocean every day.

Mending the nets. Photograph. c. 1880. LCHS Collection.

Beginnings of the Fishing Fleet

Sakonnet has been viewed as a prime fishing location for centuries. The Algonquin name for Sakonnet harbor translates into 'Fishing-Place Cove,' a term that European settlers continued to use for years. William Rotch's granting of various privileges to the Town and its citizens that included wharves and boat landing privileges at 'Fishing-Place Cove' is one indication of the importance of fishing at Sakonnet in the late 18th century. By 1838, the United States Government authorized a 400-foot rubble mound breakwater for the harbor. Only 200 feet were built, however, until 1899-1901 when the breakwater was extended to the length originally approved.[10]

Unraveling when Euro American fishermen first established a permanent presence at Sakonnet Point is challenging. Early census takers did not provide location notations for fishermen until 1900 or 1910. United States government fishing records are far more useful in documenting the Sakonnet fishing industry in the 19th century. They are especially helpful in sorting out the controversies over trap fishing. Early trap fishermen stretched long nets across almost the full width of the Sakonnet River catching everything that swam by.

The wastefulness of trap fishing was recognized as early as the late 1850s. Nonetheless, Sakonnet Point was so rich a fishing ground, and its proprietors so unconcerned about the future, that the practice continued unabated. "So long as the trapping at this locality [Sakonnet Point] is not restrained," the government noted in 1870, "the main opposers to a law at this end are indifferent, and do not care what the law is."[11]

The decline of scup at Sakonnet and other locations in Narragansett Bay was noticeable and dramatic:

> *In 1857 the trappers admitted to the committee that 60,000 barrels were taken in their traps, of which 45,000 were sold for food at 30 cents per barrel, and 15,000 for manure at 18 cents per barrel...In the year 1869, as near as can be ascertained, only about 20,000 barrels were taken; in 1870 (9,000 to 10,000 up to May 16) about 12,000, and in 1871 about the same number, or perhaps a few more.*[12]

Trap fishing. Photograph by Gus Kelley. 1935. Courtesy of the Kelley Family.

Despite the pleas to end trap fishing for scup, the practice continued well into the twentieth century. "No livelier industry is plied during May and the early part of June on the New England coast," wrote Mariana M. Tallman, a frequent 19th century visitor to Sakonnet, "than the scup fisheries about the scraggy point of Sakonnet."[13] Tallman described the excitement of seeing the boats head out from the Point to stretch their nets across the mouth of the Sakonnet.

Fishermen's Shanty. Photograph. c. 1880. LCHS Collection.

Scup were sold primarily to fertilizer manufacturers. The initial establishment of lines by the fish gangs was something of a free-for-all, with fishermen establishing claims with their buoys and traps. The method was alarmingly simple: the trap consisted of a long funnel leading to a pound (or empoundment) surrounded by at least four boats. As the scup schooled up the river, they ran through the funnel into the pound, and were hauled into the boats. The method, although effective, was certainly at odds with contemporary conservation standards, as everything following the scup became caught in the trap as well: "There may be caught in the traps besides its legitimate load, the skate, the sculpin, cuttlefish or squid, squiteague (*sic*), flounder, weakfish, sea trout, flatfish, butter fish, tautog, cunner, dogfish, sturgeon, sharks, even..." wrote Tallman.[14] She described the season as running from May until November, with horse mackerel and bluefish dominating after the scup runs were finished.

Trap fishing continues today at Sakonnet Point, although the days of stretching nets across the river to catch every schooling fish are long gone. Both conservation restrictions and declining stocks have made commercial fishing a daunting prospect.

Tallman also provided a vivid description of one of the fishermen's shacks on the Point. Virtually all surviving photographs show the exteriors of these small, wood-framed, wood-shingled buildings, often with a central doorway and one to two simple two-over-two wooden sash windows. The shacks were extremely self-sufficient, with downspouts leading to rain barrels and evidence of communal privies serving multiple shacks. Their appearance, from the exterior, is often somewhat grim. Not so, according to Tallman. Although bewailing the absence of "softening feminine touches," she described one as having:

> *...one huge unplastered room, and an open door leading into another unseen. In the first there was a huge hotel range, whereon a colossal coffee and tea-pot simmered. All up one side of the room, cool and sweet with ocean's breeze, ran a triple line of bunks, like an old-fashioned steamer's, without white counterpanes, to be sure, but with some degree of tidiness. Down the centre of the room were long benches, the board table, set with graniteware, and on it still, though fish had been consumed, bread, cheese, gingerbread, doughnuts, sponge cake, pound cake, jelly cake, and three kinds of pie.*[15]

In the 1940s, Sheila Higgins wrote a memoir of a gentleman she named 'Elsie the Lobsterman.' It provides us with a second description of a Point fisherman's cottage, and the kindly Greek who lived there alone but welcomed the many children who visited him. We don't know 'Elsie's' real name, but we do see some insights into the world of a fisherman's solitary existence:

A visit to his house was most interesting. The tiny, gray shanty was well built and showed a great deal of artistic workmanship in its latticed trimmings...At night, when he mended the nets for his lobster pots or played solitaire, old-fashioned oil lamps were his only source of light. His front porch was adorned with rare plants from Greece, and many odd seashells...

In the yard he had built a trellised grape arbor which was a sort of outdoor living room in which were a table and two chairs. A vase of flowers was always on the center of the table. For the children who visited him was provided a swing.[16]

In living memory, Dick Rogers relates a story told to him by his father about a visit to a fishing shack:

They were on stilts a little bit. But hurricanes weren't a thing then. I remember in the wintertime they put seaweed around the foundation to keep them warm. And I remember one of the stories that I like, my father was a storyteller, more than I am. He stopped there one of the mornings going down for work, and he went in to see one of the fishermen in one of the shanties. They had a potbelly stove in there and I guess it would go out during the night. My father went in there and it was cold. So my father says, "Aren't you cold?" "No," he says, "I'm warm as toast here." He had an electric blanket long before they made them. He had a wire crab pot with a light bulb in it. And he had that in bed with him. He went without a fire but with a metal pot, all he needed was a small bulb and he was warm. People had a lot of ingenuity. They could do with very little.

In addition to serving as the economic engine of Sakonnet Point, fishing also provoked occasional disputes and legislation. In April 1912, the Narragansett Real Estate Company brought suit against three fishermen (Judson C. McKenzie, William L. Winslow and George Gray), alleging that the wharves and warehouses at 'Fishing Place Cove' were built on land owned by the company. To read this case, published in the *Atlantic Reporter*, is to appreciate the long battles over access to water that have characterized Rhode Island fishing from the seventeenth century to the present.

In deciding this case, the court reviewed laws enacted by the Plymouth Colony as well as those that followed the Rhode Island charter of 1663. William Rotch's 1796 granting of rights was key. The court opined that "it must have been the grantor's intention that inhabitants of the town should exercise the privilege of building wharves, because it is inconceivable that such privileges should have been confined to the town in its corporate capacity." Ultimately, the court ruled in favor of the defendants, allowing them to keep their wharves and warehouses as a privilege by right.

Trap boats at Wickerpiece Rock, west of entrance to Lloyd's Beach.
Photograph. c. 1918. Courtesy of the Kelley Family.

Commercial fishing would remain the mainstay of Sakonnet Point throughout its development as a resort and summer colony. In the nineteenth century, fishing of all types was amazingly bountiful. In the twentieth century, the nature of fishing changed repeatedly in response to a changing environment and increased governmental control. Traditional trap fishing declined in the 1930s, as lobstering and swordfising increased. Local swordfishing disappeared in the 1970s and sportfishing declined as well, but today's commercial fishermen, including trap fishermen, gill netters and lobstermen, have adapted their methods and continue to earn their livings at Sakonnet and offshore. Their resilience has enabled them to escape the fate of fishing at Sakonnet's exclusive West Island Club.

A Sakonnet Point Tuna. Photograph. c. 1910. Courtesy of Barrett Jennings.

Visiting West Island

Hilary Woodhouse, Oral History, 2010 – When I was just a youngster, and this was probably pre-teen, maybe just early teens, we followed in my mother's tradition of going out to West Island. We would do that two or three times a summer anyway, where the drill was that, back in the early days, Harold Potter, who was a lobsterman but also the harbor master, Harold Potter would tow a number of skiffs out to Lloyd's Point and everyone who was going on the picnic that day would walk out on Lloyd's Point with their picnic goodies. He would swing the skiffs into shore, get into the skiffs and then he would tow everybody over near West Island. We would all row ashore, put our boats up, and then he would go off and we would say, 'Come back at 3:30 or 4:00.' So the day was spent out there.

I recall having barbecues and a fire would get going and then we were cooking. And swimming in the pool, and these parties were always timed when the pool was at high tide. That was very important because the pool at low tide was maybe 2.5 feet deep or 3 feet deep. High tide was 5 or 6 feet. High tide was necessary.

And then there was exploring. There were some who daringly went up the fissure, which was the crack in the rock. Of course it is still there. You could shimmy your way up. It's a terrifying event. There were some, who our parents said never did it, who did and then jumped off the west side and that was somewhat treacherous because there was a series of rocks down there that were much too close for comfort. I never heard of anyone getting hurt.

We always had these fantasies or stories about the cave on the west side. It's not a cave but when you look at it from the top it looks like it is a large, black opening that goes into the cave, where all sorts of monsters could reside. We would play war games up there, capture the flag and things like that. I can't recall exactly how these got organized except as youngsters you don't really pay too much attention to that.

West Island and Sakonnet Light. Oil painting on board. c. 1884. LCHS Collection.

East and West Islands

From the end of Lloyd's Beach, East and West Islands form the most prominent features on the horizon. Viewed from shore, the islands appear deceptively smaller than they actually are. West Island is approximately 6.3 acres and East Island is 3.3 acres. The topography of the islands is steep; the granite cliffs on West Island tower nearly 30 feet above the sea.

The islands, which have been under the stewardship of the Sakonnet Preservation Association for nearly three decades, are still popular spots for fishing, bird-watching, and even swimming. Geoff Dennis describes the approach to the islands and the excellence of the striped bass fishing:

West Island is kind of two islands…Joined by a small causeway you actually can see at low water when you cross from the inner island to the outer island, you can see the old stones, which, who knows how they moved them when they did way back years ago—beautiful nice flat stones—that were actually a walkway that you could cross from one to the other even at high water, but those have all been dislodged, probably from the hurricanes.

West Island was tough to land on. It was tough because you had to time it for the tides. It was easy to get out there if the tide was low water and you could easily walk out, but a lot of the nights I stayed late and you would have to come back with the chest waders on or you could wear shorts and hope you made it across safely…

And I caught some great big fish out there and, actually, I fished there for—it was back when I was selling striped bass—and as I said, I'd go from one island to the other to fish depending on the weather or to The Clumps.

The Clumps. Photograph by E. Atwater Byers. 1980.

Deeds and census records indicate that the islands were seen as prime fishing spots by the early decades of the nineteenth century. Surely they were lonely and remote outposts, often inaccessible from the shoreline. West Island has at least some loam deposited on it, most likely by millennia of wind, but East Island is especially desolate. Nevertheless, a small summer hotel, of which there is almost no record, existed on West Island by the time of the Civil War, as did a stone wharf.[17] A postcard from the very early 20th century shows this early small, stone hotel incorporated into the larger clubhouse.

Nicholas B. Wainwright, a descendant of one of the West Island Club's last members, has written the most comprehensive history of the club to date. In 1864, toward the end of the Civil War, the islands were purchased by New Yorkers Preston H. Hodges, Columbus Segine, and Robert S. Hone for $18,500.[18] These were all men of moderate success in New York. Unlike the Vanderbilts and others, they seem to have been more 'old money' than the entrepreneurs who succeeded at mid-nineteenth-century prosperity. Their vision was to form a thirty-person association with members contributing $1,000 each for maintenance and upkeep of the islands and their structures.

The purchase of the islands did not go unnoticed by the local press. On January 6, 1865, the *New Bedford Standard* noted that:

> *The West Island House has changed hands, having been sold to a wealthy company in the city of New York, which contemplates the erection of several cottages or other buildings in addition to the present, and also of putting up a bridge from the mainland to the island.*

Others speculated at what might happen to the islands. On March 18, 1865, the *Newport Daily News* joked that perhaps oil deposits had been discovered on West Island. Soon a construction phase put these rumors and speculations to rest, with a renovated wharf and perhaps as many as six buildings constructed on the site. Fully subscribed, the club opened for business in June 1865 for an active season that generally ran from June to October.

West Island Fishing Club. Detail from postcard. c. 1890. LCHS Collection.

Viewed from Lloyd's Beach looking southwest, the buildings occupied most of West Island. At the westernmost end were a series of wood-frame buildings described as a barn and a boathouse. The center of the island was occupied by the clubhouse itself, a two-and-a-half story, seven-bay structure with shed-roofed dormers, and incorporating the earlier West Island House. Toward the east, closest to land, was the Annex, a two-story building with quarters for the caretakers and staff.

On East Island the club maintained an active vegetable garden along with a variety of poultry and at least one or two milk cows that were periodically brought to the shelter of West Island when storms approached.

Much has been written about the captains of industry 'roughing it' on West Island. The club membership expanded from 30 to 100, according to Wainwright, and included some of the wealthiest and most politically influential men in the United States. Many were New Yorkers connected to Newport. A small sampling of Wainwright's recollection of the membership rolls includes "three Vanderbilts; Frederick D. Tappan, President of the Chase National Bank; and lastly, Elihu Root…who later served as Secretary of War, Secretary of State, and Senator."[19] Among the invited

West Island. Photograph. 1908. LCHS Collection.

guests was President Chester A. Arthur, who participated in a day of fishing in 1884. Although other presidents may have visited, Arthur's stay at West Island is the only one that can be confirmed.

The men came to socialize and to fish. The highlight of an evening's activities was the casting of lots for prime spots on the Fishing Stands.

The prime spots were those near 'the hopper,' on the southeast side of the island, where the iron stands were embedded into rock to provide secure footing. Each fisherman had a 'chummer,' whose job was to dump squid and other bait into the rocky pools. This work provided jobs for many local fishermen and remains a part of people's memories about the club into the present day.

Dock on Lloyd's Beach. Photograph. c. 1900. Courtesy of E. Atwater Byers.

Although West Island was a male domain, the wives of members were allowed to visit, along with their maids. The club also employed a variety of female servants. In 1870, Jane B. Clemis, a 42-year-old woman from Massachusetts, is listed first in the census record for the West Island Club, with the formidable title of 'Matron.'

Ever an adventuresome spirit, Mariana Tallman recorded one of the few first-hand accounts of visiting West Island. She had been advised by Mr. Slocum, the proprietor of the Sakonnet Inn, to walk down to the end of

West Island as it appeared in 1893. Watercolor by H.L. French. Private Collection.

Lloyd's Beach, wave a handkerchief toward the island and wait for the boat. On a lark, she tried it and was delighted when the boat emerged from the fog shrouding the island.

> *The club buildings, with the exception of one rather pretentious cottage, are plain, unadorned structures, mostly of plastered stone. But from the massive causeway of iron-bolted granite that bridged the outer rocks to shore, to the hen yard in the rear of the club houses, everything seemed built "for keeps."*[20]

The decline of fishing stocks off West Island began in about 1874. Having studied the meticulous records maintained by the club, Wainwright noted a peak in the number and weight of striped bass in that year—2,406 fish weighing 11,356 lbs. After 1874, the totals are disastrous. In 1886 only 22 fish were taken and by 1906, the number was down to eight. Although the members may have enjoyed roughing it, without successful fishing there was no real reason to come to West Island. Club membership declined rapidly.

The club's final season was 1906. In December of that year, the board voted to advertise the property for sale. It was sold to club member Joseph R. Wainwright in 1907, who renamed it Ardcraig and maintained it as a private fishing spot. After his death in 1917, it passed to several heirs, who finally gave the property to the Episcopal Diocese of Rhode Island in 1927. Abandoned, derelict, and vandalized, the main clubhouse and a second building were destroyed in an arsonist's fire in 1934. The other buildings may have survived in dilapidated condition until the Hurricane of 1938,

East Island as it appeared in 1893. Watercolor by H.L. French. Private Collection.

when the tidal surge finished the process of demolition. Yet as Stetson "Tack" Eddy recounts, locals continued to visit the islands for hunting and fishing:

Sometimes we would go out and shoot rats with a .22. Sometimes we would go duck hunting on the back side of West Island. There is an area there that is an inlet that is well protected in stormy weather—good for black ducks which is primarily what we were after then. And East Island—rarely ventured on that. We did some fishing off of it—striped bass fishing. I probably set foot on it but not often...You do have to be careful when you take a boat through there. A lot of people go outside the islands rather than running the risk of running aground. On the fishing front, as I said, we did a lot of striped bass fishing, too. Did a lot of night fishing with my brothers.

Doug Cory confirms that although the islands were best known for fishing, they also provided an excellent environment for shooting:

Everybody in those days went market gunning. You know, shooting birds... Yes, they would all come down and then they would go around and pick up the birds and they would take the birds and sell them and there were so many birds around...sea ducks and so forth. Old squaw, canvas backs, teal and widgeons and blue wings. It goes on and on and on.

The future of the islands was in doubt for many years and residents worried about their possible development.

There was a man who wanted to buy it and claim it as private property and my mother said, "No way. That should be kept as early Sakonnet Preservation Association." And she bought it for $1500 dollars and just left it open to whomever...That would have been sometime in the '50s. She kept it until she donated it to the Preservation Association. And it was wonderful. I mean it has this natural pool. Have you ever gone out there to swim?

Steve O'Connor, Oral History, 2011

In 1983, Jessie Lloyd O'Connor sold East and West Island to the Sakonnet Preservation Association (SPA) for one dollar. In 2009, the SPA commissioned a Comprehensive Management Plan for the Islands from biologist Carol Lynn Trocki, a plan that the SPA Board formally adopted in 2010. The plan thoroughly describes the environmental and natural significance of the islands, which are defined as Marine Intertidal Rocky Shore and Maritime Scrub-Shrub habitats covered in *Rosa rugosa*, goldenrod, and mixed grasses among the rocky outcrops. Geoff Dennis, who has volunteered with the SPA for their clean-ups and monitoring of the islands, notes their significance as a bird habitat:

I would love to spend more time out there in the fall, especially for the raptors that come through. When we were out there cleaning the island—Sharp-shinned Hawks, Cooper's Hawks, they spend a little time looking around but Northern Harriers spend a little more time and they are all coming through... I went out to the islands and, lo and behold, just inside West Island was the Snowy Owl sitting on the rock. I got some pictures of it...I did bring a few friends up in the evening on successive nights and the Snowy Owl kind of hung around there, you know, between the islands and all the little rocks in between. So that was a treat.

Dennis continues on the prevalence of the Herring Gulls, which displaced native bird species and are now, in turn, being chased out by Great Black-Backed Gulls:

I do know there are two gentlemen who have been keeping a census of the breeding birds out there every spring and I know—it wasn't this past spring. It may have been a year ago this past spring but they were out there doing their count and they saw of all things, a Red-billed Tropicbird come flying by and land on East Island...Common Eiders are nesting up there somewhere. More than likely it's on East Island. It's got the right habitat because every spring we have been seeing a hen Eider with a bunch of chicks following it around.

From what I understand, years ago, there used to be a huge rookery—I don't know if it was West Island or East Island—for Common Terns. They were displaced by the Herring Gulls, and now the Herring Gulls have started getting displaced—I don't know if by the Double-crested Cormorants, but certainly by the Great Black-backed Gulls.

Today all that remains of the club on West Island are three rough stone pillars extending skyward, a small Sakonnet Stonehenge. Thanks to the efforts of the SPA, the islands are periodically cleared of trash, monitored for changes, and thoroughly documented. The Presidents and captains of industry have departed, and all that remains are the islands themselves, timeless and eternal at the edge of the horizon.

The pillars on West Island. Photograph by Fred Bridge. 2003. LCHS Collection.

West Island

The Original Little Old Lady – As best the Little Old Lady (L.O.L.) could tell everything from the Fo'c's'le was thrown over the side. That included all manner of glass, chop and steak bones. Things must have traveled through the harbor, around the breakwater, out to sea, over to the beaches, not to mention West Island. The L.O.L. took her best friend, *Lillyputt* (an exquisite little inboard motor boat. She was all wood, with clapboard sides and teakwood trim.) and towed *Wetnose* (a real row boat) over to the island, dropped the hook and rowed in. Sadly both of these brave boats were lost in the hurricane of 1954. The *Wetnose* was beached on the north side of the island, where you stood in bones up to your knees! They were little works of art, bleached white, water worn, all shapes—actually quite beautiful! The L.O.L. thought to herself 'No wonder why so many seagulls get married and are bringing up their babies here—the dinners are gourmet!'

Geoff Dennis – Thinking about the litter clean up on West Island—why I am so gung-ho on it? I forever walked by the trash and litter out there and didn't think about it, but it's my way of giving something back. You take and take and take, which you do. You are taking enjoyment from being out there on the islands and you don't give anything back. A little bit of time we spent picking up trash—you know, it's worth it. A little good karma I figure.

Cormorants. Photograph by E. Atwater Byers. c. 1980.

After the 2006 Halloween storm. Photograph by Mike Steers.

Sakonnet Lighthouse

Perched on Little Cormorant Rock, a mere 900 feet northwest of West Island, the Sakonnet Lighthouse has withstood storms, abandonment and neglect since it was completed in 1884. Today, refurbished, painted and carefully stewarded by the Friends of Sakonnet Light, the 60-foot tower stands as a reminder of Sakonnet Point's maritime heritage, a reminder that easily could have been lost without the dedication of key individuals and the organization.

The original plans for siting the proposed lighthouse were controversial. The lighthouse, which stands a little less than a half-mile offshore, was originally intended for West Island. In a forceful 1882 letter to General J.C. Duane of the Lighthouse Board, three members of the Committee of the West Island Club, including the artist Louis Tiffany, stated their case against locating the structure on West Island. "It will be extremely disagreeable to the Club to have a lighthouse placed on West Island under any circumstances," they wrote, "and if the matter were one which the Club could decide, no money consideration would compensate for, what all the members believe, would be a very serious annoyance." Citing the proposed light's impact on the seclusion and quiet of the island, the Committee proposed that the Lighthouse Board consider the "Outer Clump." They even made some ominous threats concerning possible litigation if the Board chose to pursue the West Island location. Not surprisingly, the political influence of the club members prevailed, forcing construction on Little Cormorant.

The lighthouse is of caisson-type construction, which means that it has a massive foundation of rock and gravel that extends well below the surface of the island and below the waterline. That foundation is faced with masonry walls, and then surrounded with 1 ½-inch cast-iron caisson plates. At a height of about sixteen feet above grade is the entrance to the structure, which led to what Carl Haffenreffer described as "what was at one time undoubtedly a warm, cozy kitchen."[21] An anonymous writer in the *Providence Journal* reinforced the notion of the kitchen's homey qualities: "[the kitchen] is one whereof the most careful housewife in the land might be proud; indeed the house-keeping throughout is of the most perfect description."[22]

Sakonnet Lighthouse under construction.
Photograph. c. 1884. LCHS Collection.

Above the kitchen were the joint sleeping quarters, with a radius of only nine feet in the clear; and then above that, as one continued up the spiral staircase, a sitting room furnished with a desk, a bookcase, and a Franklin stove. Here Haffenreffer imagined the keeper at work, responding to endless requests from the government for statistics related to the wind, weather, tide and oil consumption. The anonymous 1886 visitor to the light heard the keeper's complaints about the government's request for data. "It's queer sometimes," the keeper told the writer, "what things they send us to find out about. Once they wanted us to send them word how many birds flew past the light house...Another time they asked us to tell them how many toads we see on the shore."[23]

Above the sitting room was a storage area for oil and kerosene, and higher still, the Watch Room, where spare lamps and lanterns were stored. Haffenreffer described the astounding view from the gallery around the Watch Room:

To the north, Mount Hope thrusts like a cone above the water while to the east can be seen the low purple lines of the Elizabeth Islands (fog permitting)... To the west lies Point Judith where the land, dimly seen, appears by a curious optical illusion to hang in the air without visible means of support.[24]

Finally, at the pinnacle of the structure was the Light Tower (or Lantern Room) itself, housing the Fresnel lens partitioned into white and red sections, thus creating the Sakonnet Light's 'signature' of a white light followed by three red flashes. The Lantern Room has an overall diameter of just twelve feet.

One wonders what would compel someone into a career as a lighthouse keeper. In addition to tending the light, their duties encompassed the overall maintenance of the structure, primarily chipping rust and applying paint. These maintenance activities continued as long as the light was staffed, well into the mid-1950s. But the loneliness and desolation of winter must have been overwhelming. "In the winter," writes Haffenreffer, "rough weather frequently shut them off, and they saw no faces but their own."[25]

Then there were the storms to endure, which inflicted physical damage to the structure and psychological damage to the keepers. Tallman writes:

Three winters ago [c. 1891], in a wild storm the billows arose and knocked at the doors of the lighthouse north of West Isle. They beat, and they battered and refusing to believe in the social fiction of "Not at home," burst in and flooded the kitchen, thirty feet above high water mark, and left the two keepers barren of fresh water.[26]

In an undated *Sakonnet Times* memoir in a scrapbook at the LCHS, George Neimetz, who had been a civilian worker for the Coast Guard, related the tale of a keeper (Sellers) and an assistant keeper (Fuller) who categorically refused to get along with one another. During a January storm, Fuller stepped outside, broke off an icicle measuring more than a yard long, and "laid it on the side of Sellers' neck." Sellers, who was sitting and reading next to the stove, leapt out of his chair and grabbed a butcher's knife. The two circled each other, round and round the sitting room, until Fuller's icicle melted and Sellers managed to get him out the door, which he then locked.[27]

Lighthouse keepers William and Thurman Durfee. Photograph. c. 1925. Courtesy of Carol Durfee Sylvia.

Fuller spent two days sleeping on the air compressor motors to keep warm until he was rescued by a fishing boat. As the author of the piece notes drily, "they were never placed together again." Although the story may seem amusing after all these years, it does point out the tensions and difficulties these men endured on their lonely rock a half-mile away from the desolate shore.

Perhaps the continuous crashing of waves and tides, and the cramped quarters of the light itself drove its inhabitants to take irrational actions. In 1911, the lighthouse was the scene of a daring rescue of the assistant keeper. Walter Smiley had decided to row to shore in a sixteen-foot dory. The keeper, a Mr. Manchester, had advised against it, but Smiley was determined. He had made it only about 150 yards from the lighthouse when waves breaking over the side of the dory washed the oars out of his hands. Although Manchester set off to rescue Smiley, the latter was soon in the water and struggling for West Island.

Mr. and Mrs. John Sowle were the custodians of the West Island Club. Seeing Smiley struggling in the water, Mrs. Sowle telephoned to Fall River for help. "Mr. and Mrs. Sowle stood watching Smiley make his fight against death," *The Pawtucket Times* reported, "for it was impossible to launch a boat in the high surf that was running."[28] The Sowles, both over

60 years old, waded into the water and managed to throw a grappling iron to catch Smiley as the current rushed him past West Island.

Pulling him onto the beach, the elderly couple resorted to the barrel method of resuscitation, which proved successful. By the time Dr. Brennan of Little Compton made his way over from the mainland, Smiley was recovering in bed. "The physician had little to do except to congratulate the aged couple upon their remarkable achievement," concluded the *Times*.

The lighthouse is strong in local recollection. Carol Durfee Sylvia's father and grandfather were both lighthouse keepers. She noted that Thurman Irvin Durfee arrived at Sakonnet Point to join his father William Henry Durfee, the Head Lighthouse Keeper. William stayed with the Sakonnet Light from 1921 to 1941. Thurman served as First Keeper from 1926 to 1931.

> *Being assigned to duty at the Point was very difficult. The rock was covered by the water at high tide and the men had to stay on deck and when the waves were rough they couldn't go outside because of the spray hitting the deck. They kept busy with their work keeping the light flashing and the fog horn warning the ships. The light had very little furniture, was cold and uncomfortable, even the sleeping quarters were almost bare, a small bed and maybe a chair.*
>
> *Each man stayed on duty twenty days and then ten days off a month. No family could live on Sakonnet Light but we did visit there once that I remember. Landing on the rock was difficult. My brother Richard and sister Helen jumped onto the rock and then it was my turn and I couldn't do it. My father yelled "jump" each time the dory was at the right level, finally he picked me up and threw me to Bill. Bill was quick and I soon was safe in his strong arms. All week I kept thinking, 'How will I get off this rock?'*

Both of John Morrissey's grandfathers, Calvin A. Field and John J. Morrissey, were keepers as well. Here he describes a near miss that almost resulted in tragedy:

> *My mother's father Calvin A. Field, who lived on Sakonnet Point Road, worked as a temporary Lighthouse Keeper from 1916 to about 1918. My grandmother Leila Field told us a story about our mother who almost did not*

make it into this world. She had said to her husband Calvin that she had never been out to the lighthouse and she would like to go out and see it. It was September 1916 and she was pregnant with our mother when she went out with her husband to the lighthouse. As she was getting off the skiff to get onto the lighthouse rock she fell into the water and was floating away. Luckily for my grandmother she was rescued by Grandpa and she did not drown. My mother was born on March 11, 1917.

And Randy Byers remembers a dog that made deliveries to the lighthouse:

There was on the Point, this is before the '38 hurricane, a place called McCormack's or Mac's as we called it. And it was an ice cream shop and it had little sand pails and shovels and model boats and things like that for kids to play with. And every morning the dog would swim in from the lighthouse and I think landed at Lloyd's Beach. I'm not sure exactly where it came out of the water, but he would go to Mac's and Mrs. McCormack would have the newspaper ready and tie it to the dog...anyway the dog would trot off and go running down Lloyd's Beach and get in the water and go out, so the lighthouse keeper had his paper every day.

Throughout the decades the lighthouse withstood the ravages of storms and exposure to the elements. Damage to the light from these storms paled in comparison to the devastation wrought by the 1938 Hurricane. In 1977, the *Sakonnet Times* published the memoir of William H. Durfee, the keeper of the light at the time. Durfee's riveting account, told in a laconic, matter-of-fact style, proceeds in a methodical, hour-by-hour account. Although he and his assistant keeper, a Mr. Bouley, had noted signs of an impending storm early in the day, it was only between the hours of noon and two o'clock that conditions began to deteriorate rapidly. "The sky had an amber color," he wrote, "shutting us in so we had to start the fog system." By 5:00 p.m. the sea had smashed in the roof of the engine room, effectively stopping the fog signal. By that time the lighthouse boats had been lost, the oil tank carried away and the boat landing destroyed.

At approximately 5:30 p.m., when Durfee went to light the lens, Sakonnet Point Light was hit by three successive tidal waves that submerged the tower completely. The first smashed seven deck plates out of the upper tower, 56 feet above mean high water. Durfee described the sound of the waves on the steel like that of a cannon. After managing to get the light going, he was forced to scramble through a mess of broken deck plates to get back below. The two men managed to survive the night in the light. "We wrapped ourselves in blankets, and sat side by side in the kitchen swapping yarns," Durfee wrote, "wondering when the wind would shift and quiet the sea down so we could get outside to look around."[29]

Despite their sufferings during the storm, Durfee and Bouley were relatively lucky. Farther west, off Conanicut Island in the West Passage of Narragansett Bay, the surge crashed over the Whale Rock Lighthouse at approximately the same time Sakonnet was hit. The surge swept away the light and keeper, Walter Eberle, who maintained his station until the end.

The damage caused by Hurricane Carol in 1954 proved to be the end of the light's usefulness at Sakonnet Point. James Bounakes recalled watching the storm batter the light as a young boy:

> *It got to the point where it was so far away and the wind was blowing so hard and the leaves were on the window and there was so much salt there. It covered the windows with salt. Everything was covered with salt. It was hard to see, but I could see big, huge waves breaking over the top and flying up in the air over the top of the light... You could see basically everything then, the harbor, you could see the boats going right out of the harbor. My father was saying, "Well, I don't know when she is going to go, but I guess she is going to go." But she didn't.*

The United States Coast Guard first abandoned the light, replacing it with electronic navigational aids, before requesting bids to demolish it. This request created a stir in Little Compton. Residents were eager to see the light preserved as a landmark. After four years of study, the General Services Administration determined that the light could be deaccessioned to the town, only to find that the town had concerns about the costs of maintaining it. At the 1961 Financial Town Meeting, voters decided to pass on accepting the lighthouse, rendering its demolition ever more likely.

In his 1969 essay for the *S'cunnet Scuttlebutt*, Carl W. Haffenreffer described his motivation for purchasing the light, which he acquired for $1,111 at a sealed bid auction run by the General Services Administration. "The only objective Mrs. Haffenreffer and I had," he wrote, "was to do what we had hoped the Town would be willing to do—that is, to preserve the lighthouse which for more than three-quarters of a century had been the symbol of the Town, and a lifesaver to its many commercial and sports fishermen and yachtsmen."[30] An undated *Sakonnet Times* article in the LCHS collection notes that within Haffenreffer's first year of ownership, he spent nearly $3,500 securing the light and painting it. Within three years, the structure had to be painted again, because of the ravaging effect of the elements.

Photograph. LCHS Collection.

By 1978, the Haffenreffer family decided they no longer wished to subsidize the considerable expense of maintaining the lighthouse. They marketed it aggressively to a number of local historical and conservation organizations. They even approached paint companies, offering the structure as a site of experimentation for maritime paints. Finally, the Haffenreffers found a taker in the newly-formed Friends of Sakonnet Light (as they were known at the time). This grass-roots organization was able to meet the Haffenreffer's two requests: first, that they keep the structure painted and maintained; and second, that they release the family from any liability incurred at the site. Orson St. John is widely credited as the leader of this effort, seconded by Rod Perkins.

In 1985 the Friends mobilized quickly, raising more than $50,000 and embarking on a program of painting and, more significantly, removing copious quantities of seagull and pigeon guano. The *Times* quoted Christian Finne as saying that on their arrival the interior of the light-house "smelled to high heaven."[31] The long-term vision of the group was to have the light re-lit. In March 1997, with the intervention of United States Senator John H. Chaffee, the light returned to Sakonnet after 43 years of darkness.

More recently, in 2005, the Friends of Sakonnet Lighthouse applied for and received a grant of $844,323 to support restoration efforts, which are ongoing. Today the light is largely restored, and may be the oldest structure that survives at Sakonnet Point other than the Stone House.

Thus the Sakonnet Lighthouse continues, buoyed by a loyal constituency of lighthouse supporters, preservationists, and local residents. It is fitting to close this chapter with the words of Sarah Helen Whitman's poem *Sakonnet Point.*

When, kindling through the gathering gloom,
Beyond West Island's beetling brow,
Where breakers dash, and surges boom,
We saw Point Judith's fires aglow.

Piercing night's solemn mystery,
The lighthouse reared its lonely form,
Serene above the weltering sea,
And guardant through the gathering storm.

So o'er the sea of life's unrest,
Through grief's wild storm, and sorrow's gloom,
Faith's heavenly pharos in the breast,
Lights up the dark with deathless bloom.[32]

Lighthouse

Liz Langfield – I grew up on the Sakonnet River. We summered in Portsmouth for twenty-one years. We sailed a Sunfish from Portsmouth and our goal was always the Sakonnet Lighthouse. We would turn around at that point and go back home in our little Sunfish.

Barrett Jennings – You can see the lighthouse which is as beautiful. It's just more beautiful than it was years ago. It was just a little rusty when I was a kid. But we still loved the lighthouse. I hate to say you could go out and play, because you can't really play in a lighthouse, but we did as sixteen and seventeen-year-olds. You could fish around the lighthouse. Tautog was awesome, and I have to believe it's still the same. West Island is right there. At low tide you could walk to West Island. I hope that's the way that it still is. I have been told that Lloyd's Beach, the southern portion, is no longer there, or it is cut off. Something has changed. Those were just beautiful days.

Carol Durfee Sylvia – When we visited the lighthouse [to visit my father] we usually stayed a week. We would run around the deck, play hide and seek and board games. The keepers played a lot of cribbage and made cribbage boards as a past time. I always wondered if we could sleep with the fog horn blowing, but it was amazing that the sound never bothered us. It was carried away on the winds. We would not be able to be on the deck if it was high tide because the spray would get us wet and if it was especially rough, no one was allowed on the deck. Sakonnet Light was one of the worst lighthouses because it had been built on such a small rock. It would have been wonderful to have it built on West Island where we could have had a yard and garden.

John Morrissey – My father was born on September 11, 1917 and Grandpa Morrissey was working out on the lighthouse and could not get in for a week because of a storm. During this time Grandma had Dad christened Christopher John Morrissey. When Grandpa finally got in he asked his wife, "What did you name the baby?" and she said Christopher John. Grandpa said the name was too long for such a small little baby and he said he would be called Peter. Everybody in Little Compton thought his name was Peter. Dad found out his real name when he went to the Town Clerk about 1933 to get his birth certificate.

Wintertime

Jim Mataronas – The other thing was the blizzard of '78. The wind blew probably 70, 80 miles an hour. We had the lobster boat *Sunny Jim*, our forty-footer over on Manchester's dock. That's the dock inside of the breakwater, which is Alan Wheeler's dock now. So, it got to be blowing so hard I went down there and the boat was banging so hard on the dock that I figured I would bring it over to the Yacht Club, because it was calmer. We drove the boat over and it was so rough that we couldn't even get on the Yacht Club to tie it—with the ice and everything. So we took it back, put it back on the dock. Then the snow was so high we couldn't drive home. We had to walk home, and it was blowing like 70 something right out of the east; heavy, blowing, deep snow. We got over halfway around the harbor by the right of way and Margaret said, "Oh can we stop?" I said, "No, we can't stop." She was behind me, holding on to me, and I was bent over into the wind and snow pushing our way home here to Sakonnet Lobster. When we got here the electricity was out.

The snowplows came down the next day. The tide had got so high and the harbor was frozen over so we got these big ice cakes, that were about as big as the dining room table, and bigger, and they were about a foot thick. The ocean had pushed the ice blocks up out of the harbor and across the road all the way down there by the right of way. The snowplows came down and it stopped them dead. They couldn't get through to the Point. They had to go back and get one of those big pointed plows.

Carole Davoll Flores – Certainly we were the only family down on Sakonnet Point in the winter. I'm sure the women maybe thought it was kind of lonely. We didn't see it that way. At one point there was one older couple that lived right down before you got to the docks by the name of Thayer and they lived there all year-round. He rented boats in the summer. They were there until he died and then she died. I'm thinking she was still alive in the '60s. The next closest family would be the Blades family which would be up around the corner past the Yacht Club.

Hilary Woodhouse – So we were here in the wintertime too—not full time but just for the vacation times. One thing to remember—my mother was a minimalist you know. Creature comforts were not really high on her list. She had no washing machine. She had no dishwasher. She had one little floor furnace here in the living room and a fireplace and a little space heater in the kitchen. That was the only heat in the house. She had a formula. She cranked up the fire in the morning. She got the floor furnace up, turned a little heat on in the kitchen. And then the heat rose and she opened doors upstairs and warmed up the room. But my brother always remembered the time when he had a bedroom off the kitchen. He would go to bed with a Coca Cola or something beside his bed and he would wake up and it was frozen solid in the morning. I always marveled that the plumbing would hold up under these conditions.

The Fo'c's'le on stilts over an icy harbor. Photograph. January 1955. Courtesy of Bunny Millikin.

Seaconnet Point Farm

No single person ever attempted to remake Sakonnet Point in a new image more than did Henry Tillinghast Sisson. Sisson's efforts at promoting the Point, although largely failures, contributed significantly to the Point's present appearance and land use.

The Sisson family, led by Henry T. Sisson's grandfather, Lemuel, arrived in Sakonnet Point in 1816 to become tenant farmers on the Rotch estate. Donald Gomez notes that Lemuel Sisson was the patriarch of his large Methodist family and became known for his piety and social activism. David Sisson, Henry's father, eventually became the owner of the Rotch estate and built the Stone House. Bayles, compiler of the massive *History of Newport County* (1882), also noted that the Rotch Mill was part of this estate.[33] Interestingly, a portion of a mill stone was incorporated into the masonry at the Stone House.

Henry T. Sisson was deeded his father's Stone House in 1857. After a successful career in the Fifth Rhode Island Volunteer Heavy Artillery, Colonel Sisson was mustered out in 1864 and worked at a variety of manufacturing jobs.[34] In about 1880, he developed a scheme to take his 242 acres and transform the farm into a 646-lot development known as Seaconnet Park. He proposed to rename Round Pond "Lake Josephine," as a tribute to his second wife. Some postcard views actually show the name in use, although the success of the overall development was limited. As Bayles wrote of the farm, "It is unquestionably the most valuable land property on the Seconnet peninsula. Colonel Sisson has been principally engaged for the last seven years in managing this property, plotting it, and getting it into the market as building sites for summer cottages."[35] Sisson gridded and divided the Point into hundreds of small building lots, a cottage colony to the fullest, similar to nearby developments at Island Park and Common Fence Point.

Colonel Sisson's schemes extended beyond developing the land. He needed to find ways to get his would-be buyers from Providence and Pawtucket all the way down to Sakonnet. In 1885 he launched the first steamer to the Point, the *Dolphin*, which ran for several years before disappearing from newspaper advertisements. Colonel Sisson then turned his attention to a trolley that would run in concert with the Old Colony Railroad Line.

The electric railway occupied a great deal of Colonel Sisson's later years. "At the present time," wrote the anonymous author of *The New England Coast*, "he is exerting himself to establish an electric railroad thirteen miles long to connect there with the Old Colony Railroad… Some opposition however was developed in Tiverton, and it looked as though the project would be defeated through the ultra conservation of the natives and the desire for exclusiveness on the part of some of the wealthy summer residents."[36] Colonel Sisson's Seaconnet Railroad Company, which was incorporated by an act of the Rhode Island Legislature, was as unsuccessful as his subdivision scheme. After losing the Stone House to foreclosure in 1902, he spent the last years of his life with his son in East Providence, dying there in 1910.

We may be grateful that Colonel Sisson's full development scheme for Sakonnet Point never came to fruition. Still, the effect of his plan is felt on the Point today. As Donald Gomez notes, "Many of the lots and roads plotted at this time remain today as Henry's legacy to Little Compton."[37] That legacy opened the door to future development and remains a subject of debate today.

Fortunately, several major landowners have been conscientious land conservationists at the Point in the late twentieth and early twenty-first century. As a result, nearly 76.5 acres of Colonel Sisson's development is permanently conserved with either the Sakonnet Preservation Association or the Audubon Society of RI, the Department of Environmental Management, the Little Compton Agricultural Conservancy Trust and, most recently, The Nature Conservancy of RI.

Watch House view of West Island and the Lighthouse. Postcard. c. 1910. LCHS Collection.

Watch House

A number of fine houses will be built in the very near future, the finest of which will be that of H.H. Ludd (sic–H.D. Lloyd), of the Chicago Tribune, which will be built on 'Big Rock,' so-called, the highest land on the Point, and near its extremity.

John Sargent, The New England Coast 1890

For six decades, from 1897 to 1959, the south end of the Point was dominated by *Watch House*, surely the most substantial and architecturally interesting house ever erected at Sakonnet Point. The house was the summer home of Henry Demarest Lloyd (1847-1903) of Chicago, the noted journalist, social reformer and publisher. Lloyd (HDL) was Henry T. Sisson's most, and perhaps only, substantial customer. After purchasing a number of the "Seaconnet Point Farm lots" in 1887 and 1888, HDL combined them into what would become the *Watch House* estate.

In 1951, HDL's son, Dr. Henry D. Lloyd, wrote the "Story of the Building of the *Watch House*," describing the impetus that drove the Lloyds from Winnetka, a Chicago suburb, to the New England coast. HDL, having obtained plans for the massive house from Providence architect Edmund R. Willson, went to a local builder:

By 1895 my father knew he wanted a house here, so he went to George Burgess, the old carpenter, who preceded the fellow, Herbert Grinnell, who preceded Colson Simmons, and showed him the plans, and the old fellow said, "Mr. Lloyd, I don't know as I can build a house like that, but I'll try."...The house was three years building, but they got into it in 1897, before there were any locks on the windows.[38]

The house was a sprawling, magnificently-sited wooden mansion containing elements of both the Shingle and the NeoColonial styles. The main portion of the house was flanked by two large three-story gables; a heavy shingled roof connected the gables and projected out over the main block of the house. To the east, a service wing extended from the main

Aerial view of *Watch House*. Photograph. 1930s. LCHS Collection.

block with a clipped bonnet roofline. When finished, the house was very much in character with other New England seaside villas of the time. What distinguished *Watch House* from others, was its sheer volume, and the fact that it stood alone, except for its barns and outbuildings, on a thoroughly open site.

***Watch House* interior from a 1930s rental brochure.**
LCHS Collection.

The house was designed for entertainment on a grand scale. A rental pamphlet from the 1930s in the collection of the LCHS has some of the only interior views of the house, which looks to have had at least twelve-foot ceilings. "The above illustration gives a good idea of this finely appointed summer home," reads the brochure. "The rooms are large and sunny and are completely furnished to accommodate a family desiring to entertain a number of guests."[39] A *Providence Journal* article written on the occasion of its demolition speculates on the actual number of rooms in the house. "The number of rooms in the old house is a matter of question. The rooms have been counted on many different occasions, but different records show different totals. Guests staying at the *Watch House* were assigned rooms by number so they wouldn't get lost in the great labyrinth, it was said. At last count, there were about 42 rooms in the house."[40]

Carole Davoll Flores, interviewed in 2011, is a rich source of information on the *Watch House* estate. Her grandfather (George A. Davoll) and father (Richard Davoll) were its caretakers for many years. Carole's family, and many of the Lloyd's employees, lived in homes that were a part of the estate called Wickerpiece Village. Her grandparents' home was known throughout the neighborhood as *The House on the Hill.*

And my grandfather, I assume, was born in Little Compton and then somehow got the job down at the Lloyd estate, which was a very prestigious job. That was a very, very good, lucrative job that he had. It was a wonderful job actually. And my dad worked for my grandfather. Then when my grandfather retired my father took over and did that until it was sold to Carl Haffenreffer and then my father worked there for eight years.

Really and truly we lived off that estate; between the gardens, the animals and living at Sakonnet Point where there was fish available all the time. It was a very interesting way to live. Growing up we had no clue that it wasn't ours. That's just the way it was on that estate. You wouldn't find that today at all. We had just about everything. And in the summer of course the summer people would come. They had a chauffeur and the chauffeur and his family would come. He was also the gardener. (There were) beautiful gardens at the Watch House. It was beautiful. The house would remind you of what you would see in Watch Hill today; that kind of understated wealth.

Flores described the unusual way in which workers on the estate were paid in cash.

The people that owned the farm, the Lloyds, were very, very good people and they took care of their help. I can remember back when the mailmen would come once a month with this big yellow envelope and all this money would come in this envelope for my grandfather's salary and my father's and who else would work there. They did have part-timers occasionally, like in the busy season. And I can still remember that envelope coming because I don't think you would do that today. You would never send hundreds and hundreds and hundreds of dollars through the mail. But we knew when that envelope was coming.

Gerard Dunn, supervisor of the wrecking job, praised the substantial construction of the house. He added: "*Watch House* is well built and if you wanted to live in it, you wouldn't have to renovate it. It has been well cared for, there isn't any dampness in the building, nor is the paint peeling…and boy, what a view. The location has got it all over Newport, and the beaches are sandy for miles."[41] Steve O'Connor describes the house just before it was demolished:

> *It was old. I walked through it before it was dismantled and there was plaster coming down. It was old horsehair plaster. It wasn't dilapidated. The floors weren't falling in or anything like that. It would have been a great house for an architect to dismantle and to save the timbers, because it withstood the '38 hurricane, the '54 hurricane.*

The *Providence Journal* reported on the demolition in 1959. "The destruction of the old landmark has caused mixed emotions among life-long residents of Sakonnet. One resident of S'cunnet recalled how he sat on the steps of *Watch House* and watched the American (*sic*) Cup Races of the '90s. 'They always had a houseful,' he said, 'they had a large family—all sons—and there was a lot of activity. I've heard that the old house will be knocked down,' he said with a sad tone in his voice."

***Watch House* Garden.** Photograph. 1930s. LCHS Collection.

Joan Buhrendorf attributes its loss to its failure to be adaptable to changing times:

> *It wasn't winterized, believe it or not. That was my understanding, and I believe that was true. A lot of these houses weren't winterized.*

Barrett Jennings remembers *Watch House* when he was a child:

> *Oh, absolutely. We went over. They had an auction, I think, when Dr. Lloyd died and [Chester Wilkie] ran the auction. It was a very sad day. Yes it was. It was a beautiful, beautiful home. And the flower garden I remember in the back. It was surrounded by bushes.*

Carole Davoll Flores echoes these comments on the garden:

> *They had a beautiful garden that had a huge hedge around it and it had a little small pool with a statue and beautiful flowers. I used to pick the flowers and take them to school, take them to the teachers 'cause I had so many it was just unbelievable. And we used to have 'Who could bring the most flowers for one teacher?' and naturally that was going to be me because we had a garden. So I would always win that one because they had all the flowers. My mother and a friend would go over to that garden and be in that garden when they [the Lloyds] weren't there. But that was it.*

We will give Carole Flores nearly the final word on *Watch House*, because her comments express a certain poignancy associated with both the Lloyd family and the ultimate loss of the structure. In answer to an interviewer's question whether it was true, "as the poem says," that *Watch House* was never locked, Flores replied:

> *I would believe that. To me the house was lonesome... You would never know anybody with a lot of money had this house. This house was a very unassuming house but it didn't have a warm feeling. And I don't know what that was. If you walked in there you really didn't want to live there. I can remember when I was younger... But Watch House had a different kind of an air about it... And it wasn't homey. To me it wasn't a homey place.*

The poem, written by Henry Demarest Lloyd, was kept on a wooden shingle placed on a mantle in the house.

Watch House. Sakonnet Rocks
House on the rock,
Where none shall knock.
House on the hill,
I enter at will.
House by the sea;
It harboreth me.
House of the rock,
of the hill, of the sea
Maker and Master
hold watch over thee.
Little Compton
R. I.
Sept 11, 1899.

POST CARD
CORRESPONDENCE
ADDRESS
PLACE STAMP HERE

Watch House Poem by Henry Demarest Lloyd. Postcard. 1899. LCHS Collection.

Special Deliveries

Carlton Brownell – There was an old peddler, Oliver Head, who lived on Adamsville Hill. Still had a horse-drawn vehicle. He had a very patient old horse who had a bandaged foot. Twice a week he made a round-trip of Little Compton to the Point to buy fish and then peddle it all over town. He wouldn't generally come in the house. He had a horn. He blew it, and my father would always go out with a pan to get fresh fish. And if he didn't come, we'd go down to the Point to get it.

Carole Davoll Flores – Denny and Alfred Arruda, they used to come around all the time and we always, always had fresh fruit. I think they each had a different truck. They would save things for my mother. We used to have a lot of peddlers that came. We used to have another fruit man that came out of Fall River. And then we used to have people that would come selling blueberries and things like that. I know that they did have ice around because that was Lewie Rogers that did the ice. And then we had the Rag Man that used to come. He had a horse and a wagon. You would give him rags and old clothes and I guess they did stuff with the rags. I can remember that being scary. I can't really remember what he looked like but it wasn't a pleasant thing when we knew the Rag Man was coming. My mother used to tell us that if we didn't behave she was going to give us to the Rag Man. We were petrified of him!

Caleb Woodhouse – We never locked the door to the cottage, because if we were out and the delivery truck from Wilbur's came, the delivery man would put the groceries out on the kitchen table and if there was anything perishable like butter or cream he would put it in the fridge and then depart and make his next delivery. Same way with the iceman, Dennis Arruda. He would come and have a big block of ice on his shoulder, back it up to the top compartment of the fridge, slide it in and then leave. I don't think the locks of the cottage door worked at all. In any case, if they did we never used them because we never felt we had to. It was a wonderfully carefree life.

The Sakonnet Inn. Postcard. c. 1900. LCHS Collection.

The Sakonnet Inn

Sakonnet Point's heyday lies between the construction of the Sakonnet Inn (later the Lyman Hotel/Lyman House) in 1887 and the termination of steamboat service in 1917. Others, pointing to the substantial presence of fishing industries in the harbor, extend that period until the 1938 hurricane. No one, however, would say that the Sakonnet Point of 2011 bears much resemblance, if any, to the Sakonnet Point of a century ago. The Rhode Island Historical Preservation and Heritage Commission, in its survey of Little Compton, noted the architectural losses at Sakonnet Point and closer to Warren's Point where another very large hotel called Seaconnet House once stood:

> *Few traces remain of Little Compton's earliest summer activity. The large Seaconnet House, located at the intersection of Warren's Point and Sakonnet Roads, was in operation by the middle of the nineteenth century…The [steamboat] company also operated the shore dinner hall located at Sakonnet Point and in 1887 built the ample Sakonnet Inn (Lyman Hotel), a two-and-a-half story shingled structure wrapped with a wide porch. The Seaconnet House has long been [a private home], and all the old buildings at Sakonnet Point were destroyed by hurricanes in the twentieth century.*[42]

The roots of tourism at Sakonnet Point extend back to at least the 1840s and 1850s. Few facilities existed for these early visitors, who stayed as boarders on local farms and walked the beaches and uplands. Before the Civil War, America's elite were creating new notions of leisure. The practice of going someplace and staying there for a period, although novel, was a phenomenon that had begun to shape the White Mountains of New Hampshire; Saratoga, New York and coastal New England. Not surprisingly, just as Newport began to attract summer visitors, tourists in search of a more pastoral vacation came to Sakonnet.

By the time The West Island House changed hands in 1864, the idea of visiting Sakonnet Point was well established. As Sarah Helen Whitman, a poet from Providence wrote at about this time:

> *"...people still go to Seaconnet, though, it must be confessed, that they go there under difficulties. To journey by steamboat and stage from Providence to Little Compton takes more time than it does to go by railroad to New York. Yet these very difficulties lend to the locality that charm of remoteness from the thronged thoroughfares of travel..."*[43]

Whitman also noted the surprise with which her friends and acquaintances viewed her passion for Sakonnet. "When I announced my intention to a friend in the city, he exclaimed with surprise, 'Going to Seaconnet! I thought nobody went there now.' By which he meant simply to convey his impression that, at the present day, there was no man in all that region who knew how to keep a hotel; a fact not to be disputed."[44] The lack of a permanent hotel did not discourage people from visiting Sakonnet. Most boarded with local farming families, enjoying the novelty of vacationing on a working farm, while others rented small houses and cottages.

As with any community that depends on tourism, resentments between locals and visitors occasionally simmered. In 1886, local diarist Sarah Soule Wilbour noted that a piece of property owned by one of her relatives had been sold to people from Providence. "Compton seems to have increasing attractions for Providence people," she sniffed, "I don't think it adds to our happiness to have so many city ways and fashions brought among us."[45]

But the city ways were arriving, and quickly, too. Sarah Helen Whitman saw the changes coming nearly two decades before they actually occurred:

Seaconnet, like other picturesque sea-side localities, will, doubtless, ere long
'Suffer a sea change,
Into something new and strange.'
A great hotel will perhaps rear its colossal proportions near Granny Carr's bedroom, and the haunts of the seabirds become the haunt of city belles.[46]

Whitman's predictions of the coming of a "great hotel" are almost eerie. From humble origins, the Sakonnet House grew into a majestic seaside hotel frequented by visitors from Pawtucket, Providence and Fall River. Its impact on making Sakonnet Point a viable summer enterprise was significant. Its relationship with the Sakonnet Steamboat Company and the shore dinner hall created a triumvirate of attractions that propelled Sakonnet Point into a real resort destination: one that was accessible to city dwellers and provided a variety of services for visitors.

Bayles provided the first notice of the construction of the hotel in his *History of Newport County*. At the time Bayles was writing, the core of the hotel had just been completed:

An enterprise, bearing an important relation to the future possibilities of the town, was undertaken in 1887 by a company of six persons: John Sisson, George Drowne, Frank T. Church, Valentine Simmons, John Davis, and Mrs. Doctor Cowan. Late in the fall they finished a hotel at the Point, the only one in town, which every indication shows is to be a nucleus of a large summer colony. It is known as the Seconnet Point Hotel.[47]

In its first phase, the hotel was no larger than a substantial house of the period. Measuring five bays across and three bays deep, the house was wood-shingled, defined architecturally only by a slight bit of sticking in the gable and by a veranda that wrapped around the entire structure. The word "SAKONNET" was painted boldly on the shingles themselves, announcing the arrival of the hotel era to all passersby.

Within a few years, the hotel expanded in at least two distinct phases of construction. After the first phase, completed by about 1891, the original structure had been expanded south by two additional sections, each with a wood-shingled loggia, or recessed porch, on the third floor. More significant was the addition of a tower element on the Bluff Head Avenue side of the building. The tower, an octagonal fancy, added a dramatic element to the façade but barely cleared the pitch of the roof. Although it appears to have been built as an observation platform, it became a suite.

On a later postcard in the collection of James E. Garman, the sender has drawn an arrow to the top of the tower and penned the message "This is my suite." Thus the description below is most likely from the period of this first expansion:

The Lyman Hotel with Almy's Pavilion in the background.
Postcard. c.1916. Courtesy of the Almy Family.

The house is 30 x 100 feet in dimensions, three stories in height with a tower rising from the centre front, and has piazzas ten feet wide on all sides of the first story. There are accommodations for seventy-five guests, and the rooms are all light and airy. It is well provided with conveniences, having electric bells connected from each room, bathrooms on each floor with hot and cold water, while the drainage and plumbing are excellent…The house is under the direct personal supervision of the proprietor, Mr. J.L. Slocum, who will spare no pain making everything attractive for his guests.[48]

Advertisements for the Sakonnet ran in metropolitan newspapers throughout New England. Even in distant Springfield, Massachusetts, Slocum advertised on June 8, 1891 that "The Sakonnet, situated at Sakonnet Point, Little Compton, Rhode Island, IS OPEN FOR THE SEASON. New house, within stone's throw of the ocean." Eight years later J.F. Hartwell, manager of the hotel, extolled the virtues of his establishment: "On the next point of land and in sight of Newport. First-class in every respect." Hartwell, a former resident of Springfield, continued to advertise the hotel during his tenure as manager. A 1900 advertisement noted that the weekly charges ranged from twelve to eighteen dollars, and that the "ocean view is grand."[49]

Members of the Lyman Hotel staff. Photograph. c. 1890. LCHS Collection.

Yet despite the local boosterism and the development of the hotel, change came slowly to the Point. Even by as late as 1894, there was relatively little to occupy the visitor, which was just fine with Maria Tallman. She described the *Queen City*'s landing place as a "quiet dock" with just about a dozen farmhouses (many of which took in summer boarders) in view from the deck of the steamer. After singling out Dr. Gardiner's cottage as "the most pretentious," she turned her attention to the Point itself: "praised be Allah, not a bowling alley or a merry-go-round near at hand. Nothing but a house of entertainment a little way down the grassy road, and just beyond it, a stone's throw from the red granite rocks and the tossing ocean, the Mecca of pilgrims, the Sakonnet House."[50]

The hotel's second expansion to a full build-out must have come shortly after Tallman wrote her account. Between 1895 and 1900, the hotel grew to the south by four additional sections, each repeating the architectural language of the next: a terraced first floor, large two-over-two windows on the second floor, and a loggia on the third floor with spectacular views of Newport and Rhode Island Sound. The seaward side of the first floor of this last expansion incorporated an outdoor dining area covered in an awning. Overall, the hotel stretched nearly 300 feet—the length of a football field—along its precarious perch over the sea.

In 1907 the hotel changed hands for the first time.[51] The Sakonnet Hotel Company sold the property "for $100 and other valuable considerations" to Emma F. Lyman of Boston. Emma Lyman flipped the property immediately to Thomas H. Lyman of Providence for the same price, and the era of "The Lyman House" had begun.

The lobby of the Lyman Hotel. Postcard. c. 1910. LCHS Collection.

One of the few surviving interior views of the hotel, taken during the Lyman era, shows the lobby as somewhat cramped and typical of seaside hotels of the era. The lobby has a rusticated, lodge feel to it, with wooden rockers, a rough-hewn fireplace lined with pewter mugs and teapots, and what appear to be Maxfield Parrish prints on the walls.

The connections between the Sakonnet House and Pawtucket were particularly strong. A hotel register (1915-1919) survives in the collection of the Little Compton Historical Society. Visitors from Pawtucket out-number visitors from all other places. First *The Queen City* and then the

Islander advertised in *The Pawtucket Times*. This advertising is occasionally deceptive, and often appears to be in the form of an article, rather than an advertisement. "Beautiful, cool Sakonnet Point awaits the jaded city dwellers with its invigorating ocean breezes, which sweep in from the broad Atlantic," begins one of these essays, "while seated in the spacious dining hall eating the choicest products of a real Rhode Island clam bake with all the fixings."[52] Today, not surprisingly, many people with Pawtucket roots continue to summer in, or have retired to Little Compton.

One of the last advertisements for the hotel ran in the *Springfield Republican* on July 27, 1919. It advertised "Lyman's Ye Sakonnet Inn," featuring, "Clams, Lobsters, Fish." "Don't wait until August," urged the advertisement. "Coolest place in the country."[53] After running the hotel for 15 years, Thomas H. (Tommy) Lyman died in 1922. Later that year, his executor sold the lot and hotel to James E. Lyman of Little Compton.[54] At the time the property was heavily mortgaged, but James Lyman managed to discharge the debts and keep the hotel as a going concern for a few more years.

Oddly enough, no one can say with certainty what finally finished the hotel. Some say that it burned; others that it disappeared in the tidal wave that washed over the Point in the hurricane of 1938. When James E. Lyman sold the parcel to Dr. Henry D. Lloyd, Jr. in 1929, the deed does not specifically mention the hotel or other buildings.[55] Dr. Lloyd's son, Carrington 'Cang' Lloyd is said to have saved a portion of the building and incorporated it into his home at the end of Sakonnet Point Road. The fate of the rest of the building was probably similar to other seaside hotels of the era; it likely fell into decrepitude, and was unceremoniously razed. The timing of its loss is coincidental with the Point's transformation from a seaside resort to one that was a little rougher around the edges, but nevertheless held an air of authenticity as the nation slouched through the Great Depression.

The Beaches

Postcard. c. 1915 LCHS Collection.

Joan Burhendorf – Dr. Lloyd would walk down the path from *Watch House*. He would come down to the beach and he had a pail with a thermometer in it. He would take the temperature of the water. It didn't bother him one way or the other, I think he was just curious. It didn't keep him from going in the water to swim. That wasn't a problem. I think he just wanted to know what the temperature was. Just curiosity.

Hilary Woodhouse – We sort of split our time with going to what was then Marcella's Beach but now is Tappan's Beach. It was formerly called Marcella's Beach because Marcella was the name of the Wislocki's maid and the maids used to have the beach in the afternoon and the other people had the beach in the morning.

Joan Burhendorf – Most of our time was spent very simply. You went to the beach, morning and afternoon, and then you went to the farm or you played. Mother would come back early to fix lunch. Daddy would stay on the beach. We were not allowed to go by ourselves. That sea wall was so high, and there was no sand up against it. We were not allowed to walk on that sea wall because we might fall over and it really was a good twenty feet. You don't see that today down there. It was a sandy beach. They would put a towel in the second floor window in my grandparents' bedroom. When we saw the towel we knew it was time to come home for lunch. Coming back from the beach we would run and get dressed and I would be the first one to get up in the back yard and get the hot water in the hose. That was our quick shower. Then go over to the farm and watch Dick Davoll milk the cows, and that was our entertainment for the afternoon.

The *Davis House*. Postcard by O.E. Dubois. c. 1908. LCHS Collection.

Cool, Chaste, Comfortable: The Point Develops as a Resort

With the construction of the Sakonnet House came a need to build additional amenities for visitors. This first generation of buildings included the *Davis House*, a large boarding house and restaurant; the Clam House, or Dining Pavilion, associated with the steamship lines; a Wilbur's Store Annex; and a small ticket pavilion for the steamships. Others would follow, but these were the core of the first developments.

First and foremost among these was the sprawling *Davis House* that stood opposite the Sakonnet Hotel on the east side of Bluff Head Road. Its one architectural feature was a wide porch that ran the full length of the façade. During the summer months, the porch of the *Davis House* would have been crowded with diners enjoying the lobsters and the view across the Sakonnet River.

Nearly seven decades later in a letter to the Historical Society, Jessie Lloyd O'Connor recalled the power of the sign displayed by the *Davis House* promising its guests both comfort and propriety:

Billboard inviting city-dwellers to the Davis House. Photograph. LCHS Collection.

"What a wonderful bargain was board at the Davis House! That is the same place that Miss Amey Aldrich of the class of '95 at Smith College told me had letters a foot high across the front "Cool, Chaste and Comfortable."

The *Davis House* offered visitors lodgings 'on the European Plan' and was highly regarded for its food. In addition to the house itself, the property contained several tiny cottages in the 'back lane' behind the house and its stable. A summer visitor wrote:

Rental cottage. Photograph. LCHS Collection.

Our cottage is very small, but big enough for five, since we take all our meals at the Davis House. The fare is excellent & quite reasonable… The meals are wonderful fish revelations & all the fish & lobsters & crabs & c. are fresh from the sea. I have never seen the equal & perhaps never shall again. I have already gained six pounds & each of the others is complaining of tight clothes.[55]

One Little Compton resident with deep ties to the *Davis House* is Joan Buhrendorf, who summered there from 1936 to 1958. Joan's grandparents,

Charles and Lida Winslow, rented the property from the Lloyd family once its boarding house days were through. Her descriptions of the house evoke the timeless and unchanging nature of the place:

> *It was not winterized of course. It was a wonderful house to be in. We went, and opened it up, as the term goes, May 30th and my grandmother would stay until the October 12th holiday usually…*
>
> *The fireplaces in the house were huge. There were two and they were stone fireplaces, back-to-back living room and dining room, and that was it for heat in the house—big, big living room, a huge dining room because of the table. Nothing had changed from the time that it was the Davis House. All of that furnishing was there. Dr. Lloyd never took it out, just the white iron metal beds in the bedrooms. The numbers were on the doors, on the bedrooms. There were six bedrooms on this second floor, where there was a large walk-in linen closet. And there was a large bedroom on the first floor, off the kitchen, which is where normally the help probably stayed.*

The *Davis House* managed to survive all three of the major hurricanes, including the tidal surge that swept over the Point in 1938, with no significant damage. But it was finally demolished in the early 1960s, and no trace of it survives.

Dominating most of the hastily built structures on Bluff Head was the Clam House, also known as the 'Pavilion.' This was the shore dinner hall built to accommodate those arriving on the steamship *Islander*. The Clam House was located on the westerly side of Bluff Head Road near the ferry landing. It was a long pavilion oriented north to south in the approximate location of the parking lot for today's Sakonnet Point Club. At its northern end, the building incorporated an earlier structure, which sat at a right angle to the pavilion and served as the kitchen. The Clam House was built on piers, and unlike the *Davis House*, was too insubstantial to survive the 1938 hurricane.

Another institution at the Point during the early years was the Wilbur's Store Annex, located between the Sakonnet Inn and the Clam House on the west side of Bluff Head Road. In the 1920s and 1930s, the Annex specialized in servicing automobiles. The store featured a garage with a mechanic on duty, gas and oil, and even an early rental-car agency. But most residents remember its use as a general store featuring both dry goods and fresh vegetables:

Wilbur's Store Annex. Postcard. c. 1910. LCHS Collection.

> *Wilbur's Store certainly was there and I remember Wilbur's Store used to deliver. I could remember them driving around in the truck delivering groceries to just about everybody. Then we had two vegetable trucks that would go around house to house every day. Which was neat.*
>
> *Randy Byers, Oral History, 2010*

The final significant building of the early period was the Tierney Block, located at the turn down to Bluff Head Road just north of the *Davis House*. This was an especially flimsy-looking, rambling building that was home to Owen Manchester's House. Author Martha Patten described it as providing "the best clambakes anywhere around."[56] The Tierney Block and its enormous stable were gone by the time of the 1938 Hurricane.

The Tierney Block. Photograph. Pre-1907. Courtesy of Barrett Jennings.

Shore dinners, ice cream, and clambakes: the staples of summer life then and now. By 1900 the nucleus of the Sakonnet Point resort was established. Yet the Point, although popular, remained difficult to reach. Other than the occasional brave motorist, most visitors arrived by steamboat after the brief run down Narragansett Bay.

The Islander. Oil Painting by Augusta Maverick Kelley. Courtesy of Nicholas M. Kelley.

The Steamboat Era

With the failure of Henry T. Sisson's electric railroad scheme, steamboats remained the only practical way to reach Sakonnet Point until the advent of the automobile. Sisson's *Dolphin* had provided access to the Point for a limited time. The *Dolphin* was succeeded by *Awashonks*, which burned to the waterline at its Tiverton dock on April 13, 1901. Two steamers that dominated passenger and freight trade at Sakonnet Point, and constituted the basis for many of David Patten's stories, were the *Queen City* and the *Islander*. The *Queen City*, which had been built at Brewer, Maine in 1881, ran from 1886 until its wreck in 1907. The *Islander* ran from about that time until the abandonment of the line in 1917.

Stories about the *Queen City* are linked inseparably with stories about her captain, the formidable Julius A. Pettey. Born in 1854 in Westport, Pettey lived in Tiverton. In 1900, his household included his wife and adult daughter. According to Sargent, author of *The New England Coast* (1890):

> *The following year [1886] Captain J.A. Pettey put the steamer Queen City on the route and has continued to run her ever since, winter and summer. A sail from Providence to Seaconnet on the Queen City is one of the most enjoyable that can be taken on Narragansett Bay…Captain J.A. Pettey who runs the Queen City and is principal owner is a competent*

navigator and has had a large experience in Rhode Island waters. He is a native of Westport, Mass. The Queen City…is well adapted in size and build for passing through the bridges.[57]

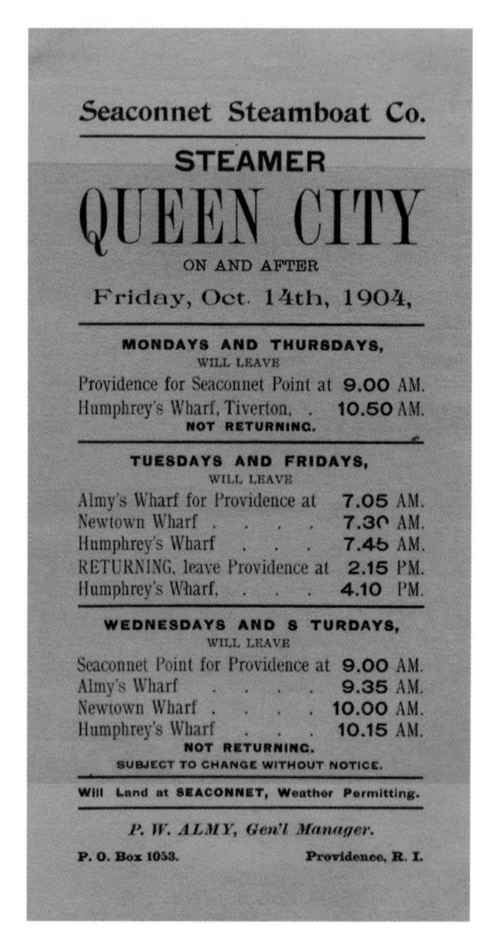

Advertisement. 1904. LCHS Collection.

Advertisements as early as 1890 boasted of the *Queen City*'s ability to make it down the river and back in a single day with time to spare: "The hours of sailing allow excursionists from Providence to go and return the same day if desirable." Petty was the owner-operator of the line, and despite his gruff demeanor, clearly took great pleasure in his vessel's capabilities. "Full of frolic the little steamer waxes now, and tilts merrily up and down the long green swells, to the singing of the wild south wind," wrote Maria Tallman in 1894.[58]

And David Patten, in his essay on Hubert Cook, the *Queen City's* purser, waxed poetic in a similar vein describing the steamer's negotiation through the visiting ships of the Great White Fleet: "In the red sunset the *Queen* came down river and weaved her way wondrously through the leviathans. And all night there was a magic of lights and in the morning the *Queen* passed them again, a midget among giants, and then they weighed anchor, wallowed around in the heavy seas and steamed away."[59]

Hubert Cook remembered Little Compton farmer Warren Kempton arriving on board every morning at 4:30 a.m. with milk for sale. "Ain't you going to get up today?" Kempton would yell to the crew. "You've been in bed so long I should think you'd warp!" But nothing compares with Patten's delightful description of the *Queen City* leaving Sakonnet Point:

> *The hawser would be heaved aboard; the cap'n, describing great arcs with the wheel, would square her around to her course; passing the end of the breakwater, and feeling the lift of the open sea, she would hoot three times; and next thing she would pass the bell buoy off the end of the Old Bull and disappear around Church's Point up river.*[60]

The *Queen City*. Photograph. c. 1890. LCHS Collection.

The *Queen City* met her end on a foggy night in the spring of 1907, running aground on the shoals near the 'Old Bull' bell buoy north of the entrance to Sakonnet Harbor. Phil Macomber, who served as a deckhand on the steamer, later told David Patten what happened on that fateful night, implying that Captain Gray had imbibed a little too much to be able to handle the boat:

> *I noticed the cap'n was carrying a bit of a load leaving Providence and with Jum McFadden on board I watched things pretty close…The cook always called for dinner after leaving Pierce's Wharf. Cap'n Gray went below with Jum, but I found out afterwards they didn't go for dinner. We got by the Bull and I got to wondering where the cap'n was and just then he came to the pilot house to relieve me and he was in bad shape…I was still below eating supper when we hit the rock…*[61]

The *Queen City* was a total loss. Macomber told Patten that "when Cap'n Pettey got there he said, 'Phil, how did this happen?' I said, 'I guess if you just look around you'll find out.'"[62] The LCHS has a copy of a broadside advertising a public auction for the wreck of *Queen City* held on April 1, 1907. The broadside, which announces the sale of the "Wreck of Hull with iron and junk," notes that the "Vessel is in 4 feet of water at low tide in Seaconnet Harbour, a short distance from the wharf—rise of tide about 4 feet."[63]

Pettey gave up the steamboat business and established a grist mill on the east side of Bluff Head Road, near the steamboat landing. Unfortunately for him it fell out of favor, largely because it ground the johnnycake meal on metal, rather than stone. The building, which later became a dance hall and then a restaurant run by Della Hayward, would eventually become known as the Casino. It was one of the many buildings on the Point destroyed by the tidal surge that accompanied the Hurricane of 1938.

The Almy Family's Clam House. Young Philip Almy is fourth from the left. Postcard. c. 1910. Courtesy of Barrett Jennings.

With the *Queen City* out of commission, the way was clear for the *Islander* to become the primary means of getting to Sakonnet Point. Between 1903 and 1917 Philip and Grace Almy ran the steamboat line and its associated amusements, including the Clam House. Mrs. Almy was the Little Compton postmistress. Every summer she moved her household from their farm on West Main Road to the Point to run the Post Office annex and the family businesses. David Patten notes that the price of the steamboat excursion included a shore dinner at the Almy's 'Pavilion.' "The boat left Providence at 9:00 a.m., got to S'cunnet at noon, left at 3," he writes. "Sundays from 400 to 500 would have to be fed, smaller numbers on week days."[64]

In addition to the promise of a shore dinner, Lloyd's Beach was a major attraction for Sakonnet's day-trippers, hotel guests, and residents alike. Originally called the *Bathing Beach*, day-trippers flocked to it in droves. Unlike the beach we see today, the beach of the turn of the twentieth century had sweeping dunes and bathhouses that could be rented for the day.

Elinor Hough recalls the attraction of the beach for summer residents who mingled with the day-trippers on summer afternoons:

> *My parents (Rachel Taylor and Dr. Harold Taylor) met down here and were married in 1915. They always said that before they were married, they had a daily parade that went down to Lloyd's Beach. They would walk down and pick up their friends along the way. I think some of them were up towards the Commons. It's a long walk but good exercise. And, of course, the Main Road was a dirt road. They would walk down to the Point to see the boat come in from Providence and then go to the beach and go swimming, because of course the bathhouses were there.*

Bathing Beach. Postcard. c. 1910. LCHS Collection.

A generation later, summer visitors continued to enjoy Lloyd's Beach:

> *We loved the beach. Lloyd's Beach is where we always swam. That was a grand time for all of us. We had lots of fun with the kids in the neighborhood.*
>
> *Joan Buhrendorf, Oral History, 2010*

All was not completely idyllic at Sakonnet. In 1909, a brief crime wave ran through the community. On July 8, 1909, *The Pawtucket Times* reported that the Sakonnet Point Post Office had been robbed, with

Lloyd's Beach. From L-R: Bruce Nourie, Joan Winslow Buhrendorf, Lois Winslow Welch, Ginny Nourie and Tiny Lloyd. Photograph. 1945. Courtesy of Jean Buhrendorf.

$1,200 and a large quantity of stamps stolen. The thieves had blown up the safe in the post office, then sorted through what was valuable and what was not. A.J. Barker's carpentry shop had also been entered, with the loss of a quantity of tools. Earlier in the week, the *Times* noted Mr. Robert Boddington's store had been broken into, with the loss of a pocketbook containing $270. Although the criminals were never caught, two local men on the way to work had seen three strangers "apparently making their way to New Bedford."[65]

Shortly after the turn of the twentieth century, speculation in cottage building accelerated. A promotional brochure put out by the newly-formed Narragansett Real Estate Company advertised "Lots on the Harbor Front/Lots on the Main Road/Lots on Hill Overlooking the Harbor/Lots on the Meadows/Lots on Ocean Front." These were small lots derived from Sisson's original subdivision. The largest, on the ocean front, measured 15,000 square feet (a little less than one-third of an acre) and the smallest, overlooking the harbor, were 8,000 to 10,000 square feet. Most of the houses illustrated in the brochure are simple, one to one-and-a-half story bungalows.

Construction at Sakonnet Point was modest, and used a seaside vernacular defined by natural materials blending horizon and seaside in a seamless fashion. The aggressive nature of the marketing campaign makes us wonder if even by the end of the first decade, Sakonnet Point was beginning a slide into obsolescence as a resort. In a postcard from about

1910, the Narragansett Real Estate Company has erected a large billboard on the west side of the harbor (easily visible from the steamship landing) reading "SEACONNET LOTS/EASY TERMS/REDUCED PRICES."

The *Islander* made its last trip in 1917 and, with the end of the steamboat line, the hotel and Clam House went into serious decline. The start of World War I, the beginning of Prohibition and the advent of the automobile all coincided with the last days of Sakonnet Point as a resort destination and signaled a shift in the way Americans viewed leisure and recreation. The vast majority of day-trippers were gone but Sakonnet's summer families were here to stay.

Postcard by O. E. Dubois. c. 1910. LCHS Collection.

"Boys, Time to Drive to Sakonnet!"

Betts Woodhouse to her sons in the 1930s and '40s

Photograph by E. Atwater Byers. 1981.

Caleb Woodhouse – Well, I first came as a boy in the 1930s when Tom, my father, and Betts, my mother, would rent cottages around town for a couple of weeks one time every summer. We would drive up from New York, an eight-hour drive, and get here and stay. The cottages were located all over Little Compton, but for some reason, my mother always called it "Sakonnet."

Hilary Woodhouse – I must have been six, or five, I started coming here with my brothers for the summertime and in our family, my oldest brother [Caleb] was a tennis player. That was his passion so we never saw him. He went off and hit tennis balls all day and my brother Bri was a golfer and I never saw him. He played 18 holes in the morning and in the afternoon. The conversation around the dinner table was always about out of bounds and in bounds and ids and oobs, Goodrich putts, and so forth. I spent my time as a youngster at the harbor. First of all, just fooling around at the Yacht Club doing all the things that kids do today: crabbing, rowing, fishing for minnows and all that good stuff, but eventually started to sail. I have my first sailing trophy from 1947, when I was ten years old, of the Wednesday series. I came in first or second, in the Beetle Cat class. That's what the summer was all about.

Caleb Woodhouse – The fish came almost directly because the fishermen would take a break from that net mending to watch my mother Betts, an artist, do her sculpting. They would be out there standing hour by hour in the fields mending nets. And they would look at Betts with her clay and say, "Oh, Mrs. Woodhouse, I would never have the patience to do that." But in gratitude they would occasionally drop off fish. The fishermen were very nice to us.

Hilary Woodhouse – I had found an anchor, one of those plow anchors on the dock and I tied it to a line. I was throwing it in and pulling up stuff on the bottom and seeing what I could catch and throwing it in again. I was having a pretty good time when I threw it in but the line caught around my shoulder and threw me into the water and I was obviously surprised but I tried to swim up to the surface and I couldn't. The anchor was holding me down and I could get my hand out of the water but I couldn't reach the top of the float. I tried and I tried and I'm holding my breath and holding my breath and I finally said, 'Okay, this is a tough way to go but you know, so be it.' And I just relaxed and sort of went down to the bottom. And I said, 'I might as well try one more time.' The line had slipped off my shoulder by relaxing and I shot out of the water. Well, needless to say, I'm running home sopping wet and I pass my brother on Round Pond Road. He is going off to some place. I said, 'Bri, Bri I nearly drowned.' And all he did—he didn't break his stride at all—he said, "Well a miss is as good as a mile." And he kept walking. I never admitted to my mother what had happened.

The Second Maid's Story

Inger Ormston, Oral History 2010 – Coming down for the first time the roses were just in bloom on the stone walls and the trees formed an arch on West Main Road. I was very impressed. It was 1937 and I was 17. I came to New York by bus from Iowa to work for the summer and then I was to return after the summer to Iowa to finish my high school education. A chauffeur of a Mr. and Mrs. Alexander Royce brought my aunt and I down to work at their home for the summer in a limousine. And that was also very impressive

I was second maid at the Royce House (10 Minnesota Road). I made beds, served hors d'oeuvres for their cocktails. Kind of an all around girl—ironed, cleaned. I got $35 a month plus room and board. And I was glad to get it because that was more money than I would have gotten back in Iowa.

The view was so beautiful, never having seen the ocean before. I was very impressed by all the boats and the yachts. The Royces had a fifty-foot yacht. And they had a long dock in front of their house. It went way out and it was very nice to go there and get put on a rope, because I couldn't swim.

We didn't go to Lloyd's Beach because we were working. We did get a day off to go down to Warren's Point one time because they were members. The chauffeur took us down and came down later in the afternoon and brought us back. You didn't go to the city. We stayed right at the Point. We didn't know there was even a Commons at that time.

Saturday nights, the maid in the next house, my aunt and I went down to Anne's Cove. They had a band. They had shows sometimes, not always. I met Eddy at Anne's Cove. Eddy came in on a catboat, and came over and asked me to dance. When I came back in '39, then it was kind of a date, if he came in by boat. He and his friend would take us out for a ride in the afternoon but we had to get back because we had dinner to serve.

Rum-running

The Prohibition era, which began with the ratification of the Eighteenth Amendment in 1919 and ended with its repeal in 1933, proved to be less of a burden for residents of Little Compton and more of an opportunity to make a little extra money on the side, especially during its later years as the United States slid into the Great Depression. In an editorial note to Wilbour's *Notes on Little Compton*, Carlton Brownell confirms this notion of Prohibition as employment opportunity: "The editor's father was then Senator from Little Compton and believed people favored prohibition not because they opposed intoxicating beverages, but because prohibition provided well-paying work in a rural town where jobs were scarce."[66]

Carole Davoll Flores agrees that Prohibition offered job opportunities for the residents, although not everyone was able to take advantage of those opportunities:

> *During Prohibition my father and his three brothers were offered a job at night down on the docks. I'm sure it was loading the contraband or whatever. So they snuck out of the house at night. Of course my grandmother was right on them. She went right down to the docks. Did not care who was there with their submachine guns hiding up in the whatever, because I understand that was going on, and she grabbed the four boys by the ear and said "You will go home!" My father said it was the most humiliating thing he'd ever been through in his life. He said all he wanted to do was work one night and be able to buy a car but she was having no part of that. Al Capone or no Al Capone, she was right down there and grabbed those guys 'cause they were very young, probably around 16ish, and they were all very close in age. I just think that was funny.*

Often the only official records of rum-running during Prohibition are newspaper accounts of arrests and searches. James E. Garman, in his *Tales of Newport County*, provides a comprehensive overview of rum-running in

Newport County. The system of moving banned alcohol into New England was straightforward. Rumrunners from Canada and even Bermuda anchored offshore on 'Rum Row,' outside the three-mile limit. Smaller, high-speed craft from places like Little Compton would meet the vessels and load the cargo. Once on shore, the alcohol would be transferred to trucks and moved across the countryside. Certainly there was little stigma attached to rum-running. As Dick Rogers notes:

If my family did it that made it respectable. You got to put it in the right context. No, certainly my family did it. That's where my family got its start financially…Well the boats came in a lot of places but most of them were from Canada and they would anchor offshore cause with the three-mile limit it wasn't that far out. And people with boats would go out, right, and bring the booze in to different beaches. Anywhere. They just brought them in anywhere. Then it would be hidden for later deliver…And they would put it in a cistern for example. Pretty open.

Prohibition and rum-running are still alive in the memories of Little Compton residents. Andrea Phillips related a story about her husband, the late Bud Phillips:

Bud went out one morning and was down playing on the beach and was a little kid. And he came upon all these bottles of presumably bourbon or something illegal all over the beach. Some of the rumrunners must have just unloaded them to, you know, if they were getting followed or in trouble or something. So Bud got rocks and broke them all because it was fun. Well, he went home apparently and told his dad "Oh what fun I had breaking all these bottles down on the beach." And his dad was like "You did what?! Do you know how much I would have liked that!"

And Dick Rogers' father remained cool, even in the face of federal agents raiding his house for cached liquor:

I'll give you one more so, 'cause I remember as a little kid, I was pretty young then. I heard a truck out in the yard and I remembered saying to my mother, 'What's that?' She said, "Oh, they're delivering coal." I didn't

> *know until years later they were delivering booze. Well, at one point they had a raid. They came to the house and they found the liquor (usually there's somebody telling). So they're loading it and putting it in the truck and my father had kind of dry, but very witty you know what I mean. And they're taking it out and he says to them be sure you get a good count so when you bring it back. And they said, "You don't have to worry about that." Well the people financing this operation had good lawyers, the judge found it was an illegal search and they brought it back.*

With the repeal of Prohibition in 1933, opportunities for money making withered away. Still, the Point was a remarkable place in the 1930s; a little less picturesque than it had been in the 1890s, a little more down at the heels, but nonetheless a vibrant, living community filled with remarkable characters.

Prohibition was an opportunity for many local families to get ahead. Photograph. 1932 Chevrolet. LCHS Collection.

Sakonnet Harbor. Photograph by Gus Kelley. 1935. Courtesy of the Kelley Family.

Fishermen's shanties and *The House on the Hill.* Photograph. Courtesy of Barrett Jennings.

Before the Storm

According to the 1930 census, pre-hurricane Sakonnet Point was home to 125 people. Demetrius Mataronas was one of them. He arrived in America in 1918 and was described as a fisherman living with his wife and his nine year-old son, James. Building No. 337 on the census schedule may be Grinnell's fishing shack. Living there were seven Nova Scotians including Edward A. Hamilton and his wife Carrie, Maynard Blades, and others all described as 'trap fishermen.' Other Nova Scotians included the Hines family and Reverend George Reed of the Congregational Church in Little Compton.

As more and more immigrants arrived in the early twentieth century, Sakonnet Point began to reflect the larger idea of America as a melting pot of different nations. In addition to Yankee, Greek and Nova Scotian families, we see other nationalities. John J. Morrissey, the former lighthouse keeper, and his wife Bridget are listed as having emigrated from Newfoundland in 1911. Azorean Manuel Sylvia, his Swedish-born wife Hilda, and their son Victor, were all involved in the fishing industry. Also listed are Frank Rosa, a gardener from the Azores and his extended family; and Manuel Gomes, a farm laborer who was born in America but whose wife Quiteria arrived from the Azores in 1916.

Census takers counted 75 different dwellings at the Point. Twenty-six of the 125 residents were either trap fishermen or lobstermen. Relatively few were listed as employed in anything related to the tourist trade. No restaurant owners, no ice-cream parlor owners, no dance hall proprietors. This tells us first, that very few of the owners of the Sakonnet Point attractions lived at the Point. They may have lived in their shops and restaurants for the season and then returned to homes and jobs elsewhere. Second, the majority of people who worked in Sakonnet Point businesses must also have been seasonal. This suggests a typical 'tourist town' phenomenon, with the population swelling from June through August and then shrinking over the winter.

Although the large-scale resort era died out with the Lyman Hotel, people still came to Sakonnet. If the Depression Era Point attracted a different clientele, it was because the attractions had changed and were now a little rougher around the edges. In every way, the Point was a reflection of the times: a destination lined with restaurants and small stores, and a place where even during Prohibition, you might find a discreet place to enjoy a quiet drink.

An aerial photograph of the Point before the 1938 Hurricane and its annotations by local residents, are worth studying closely to understand what was lost in the storm, as well as what had already been demolished, abandoned, or razed prior to September 21, 1938.

In the photograph, three key structures are missing or just out of view. These include the Sakonnet Inn/Lyman House, the *Davis House*, and the Tierney Block (home of Manchester's restaurant), all important elements of the Point at the turn of the twentieth century. We know that the *Davis House* survived well into the late 1950s or early 1960s, but what exactly happened to the other two remains a mystery.

Along the south side of the harbor, directly on the beach, were approximately nine or ten fishing shacks. All were modest, small wooden structures located between the high-tide line and the road. The exception was the huge, barn-like structure used by Grinnell's Fishing Gang, at the corner of Bluff Head Road. Dick Rogers describes these communal structures in a recent interview:

The fish companies had a building down there and the fishermen would live there. Now they did that up until 1944, I think it was. For the summer when they hired the help they'd bunk, probably worse than a college dorm. They had an open room, put a whole bunch of bunks in there and the fishermen lived there.

As you turned the corner and headed toward the Point, the first structure you passed on your right was the modest store/restaurant of 'Tony the Greek.' Opposite Tony's was George Thayer's tiny restaurant. On your left, you then passed Wilbur's Store, the former Almy Place, Irving Wilcox, and Mack's Store. After Mack's Store came the sprawling extent of the Clam House, built out on wooden piers over the shoreline, and at the very end, the small one-story collection of buildings making up the Marcus Wilcox (or Bluff Head) fish market. The restaurant owned by 'the Greek' is the subject of a humorous recollection by Carlton Brownell:

It would have been my sister and friends of ours, the Wilburs: Barbara Wilbur and her brother Champ. And we went in there one time to get hot dogs, I think. And Barbara spoke to him very nicely as Mr. DaGreek. Because she thought that was his name.

The photograph clearly shows the dilapidated former ticket office for the *Islander* standing on the wharf between the Fish Market and the Mill House/Casino, which had served a variety of purposes over the past three decades. Returning along the harbor side, one passed the Rope and Net Shed, the Barrel House, and two small residences before returning to Tony the Greek's at the top of the road.

Not one of these structures survived the 1938 Hurricane. Although the Point may not have been "swept clean," as described in some accounts, its infrastructure was obliterated by wind and tidal surge. The tales told by Little Compton residents of the storm serve as a poignant reminder of the fragility of Sakonnet Point, and its precarious position at the edge of the ocean.

Sakonnet Point before the 1938 Hurricane

Structures Lost During 1938 Hurricane

Photo taken between 1933 and 1938—Building identification by Augustus Kelley, Helen Ward Moore, George Metayer, Lois Almy, Dorothy Almy, Vivian Grinnell LeBeau.

1 Gray's Store

2 Ross Simmons

3 Bill Briggs

4 Harold Potter

5 Tom Morrissey

6 Ross Simmons' boat Elaine

7 Grinnell's Fishing Gang

8 Site of the "Tierney Block"

9 Tony the Greek

10 George Thayer's Restaurant

11 Beach right of way

12 Wilbur's Store

13 Frank Irwin Ward (formerly Almy)

14 Irving Wilcox

15 Mack's Store

16 Clam House

17 Marcus Wilcox Fish Market

18 Ticket House

19 Mill Store (formerly Hannah Elizabeth's Tea Room (Della's), Casino, gristmill)

20 Rope & Net Shed

21 Barrell House

22 Nina Blades

23 George Thayer

24 Telephone poles (only things left on the Point after the storm)

■ Landings

Courtesy of Lucy O'Connor.

Vanished

The Steamships

Carlton Brownell – They really shipped a lot of stuff out of the Point. Potatoes were a big thing. The farmers put their potatoes down there on the boats to go to Providence. And all along the water there were the wharves that you could go out and get on. I remember my father always said the first bathtub we had here in the house came by boat to the Point and was brought up about the time I was born, around 1917.

The Lyman Hotel

Carlton Brownell – Lyman House always was able to serve drinks. I think David Patten in one of his stories mentions how the local chief of police never knew there was a room in the back. He didn't know there was a place he could get a drink. They always had a shady, but seductive call to people. More to young people, of course. My grandfather, my mother's father, he owned a large part of that at one time. But purely a business. And I don't think it was ever as financially successful as some harbor towns and fishing towns. It was kind of seasonal, very seasonal.

The Fo'c's'le

Nate Atwater – Oh, the fritter story! I'll never forget that. That was wonderful. It was back in the '50s, and we were in there one night—it was between seasons, it was not summer and it wasn't fall, but it was headed towards fall. There weren't too terribly many people in the bar that night. Mike Rogers came in from out back—it was getting near the end of the evening, and he said, "Okay boys, eat hearty," and he gave us a big, big platter of fritters. Then he walked back into the kitchen. I was there with Bud Phillips, and I noticed this long, lean but brawny arm with a tremendous hand attached to the end of it—reach out, and grab a fritter from the platter. And seconds later, I heard a splat. And that fritter wound up right on the side of David Brayton's head, he was down at the end of the bar talking to somebody. And with that, the next thing you know…the whole place is flying with fritters! Finally, Mike came out, and here's this mess, and all these things flying through the air, and Bud was sitting there, looking as innocent as a lamb! With that, "Who, me?" expression on his face!

Fisherman's Shanties

Inger Ormston – Where the parking lot is now for the fishermen's dock, at that time there was a building there where the fishermen lived that worked for Holder Wilcox. That was where the fishermen lived and they had a cook. I don't know why that stopped—them living there, but my aunt and I rented that building and ran it as a Galley and rented across the street from George Thayer to live. Our family and then my aunt had a room off the end of that building which was probably where the cook had. When the fishermen couldn't go out they would gather in the morning and drink coffee by the gallons and tell all kinds of stories and get everybody all riled up.

The Galley

Inger Ormston – The Galley was '49, '50 and '51 and then we gave that up because we weren't making much money. My aunt and I had various of the local girls working for us and Eleanor Carroll happened to be one of them. The other locals I can't really remember. Only Eleanor is very prominent in my mind. From 6:00 in the morning until about 9:00 at night. It was long hours and very small pay. Of course we couldn't compete with the Fo'c's'le, really. We had chowder and clam cakes and homemade pies. My aunt was a marvelous cook. She made donuts. The food was good because my aunt was a very good cook but the hours were too long for the expenses—what with renting two buildings it got to be a little bit too much.

St. Andrew's By the Sea

Agnes Langdon – The Rev. George D. Langdon, headmaster of the Salisbury School in Connecticut, served as the summer minister of St. Andrew's by the Sea from 1936 to 1952, excepting several war years when the school ran during the summer. St. Andrew's, founded in 1914, was located on Sakonnet Point Road, on a lot just north of the Stone House.

Rev. Langdon and his family lived in the rectory close to the church building. They loved the neighborhood, a stone's throw from Round Pond, in walking distance to the harbor and to the beach, called Gardiner's Bluff after the great brick house on the road just before it dips down to the water. All enjoyed summer life in Sakonnet. They belonged to the golf club, yacht club and Warren's Point beach club. The children, George and Mary Anne, walked to the club daily; they played good tennis and golf , winning championships occasionally, and George Jr. loved the water; sailing and fishing. The harbor was a favorite place to hang out, one could buy fish from the fishermen there and perhaps be taken along on a boat.

St. Theresa's Catholic Church

Margaret Mataronas – I have recollections of being a young girl and my grandmother, Lillian Shepard Rosa, would tell me that, as a young girl, she, herself, lived down on Bluff Head Avenue area towards Lloyd's Beach. Her mother was a housekeeper for the Fish and Game Club out on the island. There was a little church (St. Theresa's) here on the Point in those days. One day some men were moving the church back up the road. My grandmother said she never saw her mother run so fast after them as she did that day, because she had hidden her money in the church!

John Goulart – They built a church—St Theresa's. Well I think that was built for the pot whallopers anyway. Those were cooks. There were a lot of cooks—women—mostly Irish. It just seemed so every summer person that owned a house there had a cook and housekeeper and maid. Don't see those today at all.

I can't think of the girls' names, but they were summer people and they were sisters. Well, tell you where we used to meet them at the church they tore down at Sakonnet Point. I used to go down there for Mass in the summertime. They were very fine...they were summer ladies. They had a gift shop near the Fo'c's'le on that side. They were Irish girls.

1938 Hurricane Quilt by Augusta Maverick Kelley. Each decorated panel represents a consequence of the storm. Courtesy of the Kelley Family.

Lloyd's Beach after the 1938 Hurricane. Only two walls remain on West Island.
Photograph. LCHS Collection.

Hurricane of 1938

Sakonnet Point is gone.

Frank Goulart to his son John, September 22, 1938

No event caused more irreversible changes to the landscape, culture, and economy of Sakonnet Point than the unnamed hurricane of September 21, 1938. The storm, which caused cataclysmic damage and as many as 600 deaths throughout New England, was all the more disastrous because of the lack of early warning systems.

Despite the absence of radar and communication through mass media, people remembered a series of omens that morning which seemed to suggest that this would not be a normal day. In 1939 the *Providence Journal* ran a fascinating article describing a meeting the Little Compton Historical Society held at the Fo'c's'le on July 17 of that year. At the meeting people spoke of the strange premonitions experienced by birds and beasts in the area: cows getting up, lying down, and getting up again; wild ducks circling in the sky; and no other birds heard on the day of the storm. Mrs. Herbert Taylor noticed "the skies darkening and the wind's roar with a sound never heard in these parts. Then came the wind, then the black mounting geyser, and then the crumpling of buildings."[67]

The lack of warning resonates in many accounts. Fred Torphy, relaying tales heard from Gus Bounakes, describes how people fled to *Watch House* for safety:

> *...absolutely no warning in '38—they were on the Point and everything picked up and the water came up and across the road. No one—it happened so quickly—no one could get out and around the Point back toward where let's say the cove and the Yacht Club was. So they went up to Lloyd's house, which was Dr. Lloyd's, which was near Lloyd's Beach. The house is no longer there. It was a great big old house, it was up there. I remember the Lloyd House. Gus Bounakes told me—he said there were 30 or 40 people because the people had come out from the Point who worked on the traps and they ran up there to get some shelter. And I asked him, I said, 'What happened? What is your memory about the tidal wave?' And he said, "Well, it really wasn't a wave, as such. The first thing I knew that something was happening," he said, "everybody in Watch House started to scream. I looked down toward the south. That would be toward the lighthouse further south than the lighthouse, maybe a mile or two." And he said, "The sea just rose up. It looked like the whole horizon had risen and was coming toward the land." And he said, "We really didn't think we would survive it."*

The harrowing experience of the keeper of the Sakonnet Lighthouse indicates that the peak of the storm was between 12 noon and 5:30 p.m. Keeper Durfee later wrote his account of the storm:

> *By three o'clock the wind blew a gale and the sea began to go higher and higher. Pounding with such a force that it smashed up all the boats and by four o'clock we had lost part of our rain shed, one oil tank, a boat landing, also smashing in the engine room and flooding the engines and putting the fog signal out of commission. At five o'clock all outside doors had been carried away and all windows from the first floor to the third floor were stove in, so that we were practically flooded out of our home. At five-thirty I went into the tower to light up. While there, we took what was called a tidal wave. There were seas that went by that completely buried the tower. The*

first sea that came along was the one that caused the most damage. That one broke seven plates out of our upper deck, which is fifty-six feet from the average high water. That sea, when it hit the tower, sounded like a cannon. And it hit with such a force as to knock me off my feet...But when I finished lighting up and started to go downstairs I was some surprised to find that I had to crawl through some broken deck plates that had fallen over the stairs. At sunrise Mr. Bouley put the light out and called me to see the beach. And we were surprised when we looked to the Point and saw that everything had been washed away.

This timing agrees with most accounts of the storm, which describe landfall at Westerly, Rhode Island at 3:50 p.m. and a subsequent storm surge of 15.8 feet up Narragansett Bay and the Sakonnet River. The giant wave (or waves) swept across Sakonnet Point, leaving few structures in its wake. Randy Byers describes the shock of encountering the devastation:

And we got as far as Tiverton and the National Guard was out. And we had to go to the Tiverton Library and stand in line for a long time to get a permit to go to Little Compton. And we came down and I was absolutely shocked when I looked at Sakonnet Point. They wouldn't let us any closer to the Point than the corner before the Yacht Club. And my mental picture was looking over at the Point itself and seeing just telephone poles and one roof. There was nothing else on the Point. It was all gone.

The most tragic occurrence at the Point was the loss of Grinnell's fishing shack, in which ten fishermen had hunkered down to ride out the storm. Four of the occupants died in the storm. Allen Kimpel, a survivor, told the *Providence Journal* that he was in the shack "when the tidal wave took off our part of the building and flung us into the river."[68] With the shack adrift in the Sakonnet, Kimpel looked for anything to grab onto. Spotting the fishing boat *Wahoo* adrift, he leapt for the boat's mooring line. Contact between the shack and the boat briefly crushed Kimpel, who emerged with a badly-cut face but managed to scramble on deck and start the motor. He picked up three of his companions but four, Al Sabins, Ebenezer Keith, and Mr. and Mrs. Vasco Souza, were never seen again and presumed drowned.

Carol Durfee Sylvia recalls this tragedy and her other experiences from the 1938 hurricane:

We lived in my mother's family home at Sakonnet Point. There were two houses and a two-car garage behind a large hedge; both were lost in the 1938 hurricane but the garage survived. We were in school when the storm hit. When the water came up to the doorstep they decided it was time to leave. When they were in the car, a man came on horseback and knocked on the window and told them people were going to the Lloyd's house for safety. While they were there my aunt would go up to the windows to watch the destruction of the different houses that were being swept away. My mother was too frightened to watch as familiar homes were being swept away.

When school was out we got on the school bus and headed up Meeting House Lane for home when we came to a tree across the road. The senior girls shrieked but my brother calmly said we could get home another way. He always saved me a seat on the bus. On the way through South of Commons Road to Swamp Road we ran into another tree down. We ended up staying at Mrs. Wilbur's (my third grade teacher) house for the night and she let us stay up until 11 p.m.! The girls stayed in a bedroom but the boys slept on the floor in the attic. The next day we went to school and my mother came in to my classroom to be sure I was okay.

Fred Torphy was told the story of Grinnell's fishing shack by Gus Bounakes:

And when the tidal wave—it was more of a surge—when it hit around Lloyd's he said it swept everything with it, small houses around this big Lloyd house went—horses, cows. And then he said it went down towards the Point and it took everything with it, including—he said some people—a few people had gotten on top of a trap building, a building that was used for the trap boats and the nets. And he said that building got swept out with people on top of it. And he said he saw someone jump onto boats in the harbor and I'm not sure how many people were lost and not lost, but he said he and everybody in the Lloyd House didn't expect to live through it.

The Providence Journal reported the catastrophic results of the storm to Sakonnet Point. "Sakonnet Point bore the brunt of the blow, the tidal wave leaving the breakwater clean of buildings and practically leveling the cove," reported the paper. "More than 100 persons were made homeless, and about 45 buildings, including stores, dine and dance places, and homes, and fishing shanties destroyed."[69] The harrowing story of Mr. Sylvia and his daughter was noted. Huddled in the house of Mr. and Mrs. Charles Gray, the Sylvia's and the Gray's houses were swept into the Cove by the tidal wave before the surge returned the house to the ground just next to its foundation.

Extensive photographs depict the destruction at the Point. Cars flung into the water like toys; buildings smashed or dumped into the harbor; downed utility lines and wreckage everywhere. That there was no greater loss of life is, in retrospect, amazing. The reconstruction began in earnest, but it would be less than a decade before a second catastrophic storm smashed through the Point.

1938 Hurricane damage. Photograph. LCHS Collection.

The Summer Colony

Carlton Brownell – The automobile really changed things. You know boarding houses were great things in Little Compton. Almost every farmer, if his wife wanted to do a little more money-making for her own, she'd be able to run a boarding house. Boarders would come for a week or two weeks. The women and children would come for the week. The husband would come down weekends. They would come through the Tiverton train station. There were jitneys, as they called them in those days, in stages would pick them up and bring them to the boarding house. But that all ended when people began getting their own automobiles. That's when the big summer colony started. Because the first summer people were mostly quite wealthy. They all bought farms and even kept the farms running by just coming occasionally.

Barrett Jennings – I remember going (in the 1950s) with my uncle Phil Almy. He was on the Star Route and he worked for the postal department too. We would deliver the trunks of the wealthy people that lived in Sakonnet, around Bailey's Ledge and pretty much at the Point, where the Yacht Club is. That area there, we would, for a month when I would go with him, we would just take these trunks—I really wasn't that strong. I was a kid. But he would do that.

Rod Perkins – I am the 10th generation in my family to have lived all or part of the time in Little Compton.

Carlton Brownell – When the summer people began getting their own cottages, then tea rooms became the big thing. I think every young woman who graduated and hadn't gotten married got her own tea room.

Fred Torphy – Oh, we would leave right after Labor Day because when I was a child it was kind of a tradition. Everybody packed up and basically left because the houses were not winterized. School started. Most families, as opposed to today, they wouldn't stay after Labor Day. Everybody would leave.

The *Marsh House*. Photograph by Blackmer Humphrey. Courtesy of Pam Carter.

The Kelley Family Summer Home. Photograph courtesy of the Kelley Family.

"Ma" Hines at The Fisherman's Ball. Photograph. c. 1945. Courtesy of Walter Elwell.

The Last Fo'c's'le. Postcard. c. 1972. LCHS Collection.

Rebuilding the Point: The Fo'c's'le's Heyday

Despite the stunning level of destruction from the hurricane, an attitude of optimism prevailed at Sakonnet Point. Within a year, an extensive bout of construction had created a new Point. "The Bluffs is built up again, bigger and better than ever," reported *The Fall River Herald* in 1939. Photographs accompanying this article supported the contention that, "The new buildings are an improvement on the old and the structures are more firmly secured." The highlight of the series is a photograph of the new Fo'c's'le and bowling alleys. "Activity at the Bluffs is shown by the numerous automobiles in the picture," the article points out helpfully.[70]

With the resurrection of the buildings at the Point came a new era, that of the summer colony. The Point was just rough enough around the edges to appeal to a wide range of people, including urban dwellers seeking sanctuary from the city, artists and intellectuals, and fishermen. During World War II, soldiers added to the mix due to the military presence at Fort Church. The central meeting place for all of these different people was the Fo'c's'le restaurant, owned by the Rogers family. The Fo'c's'le had started in the former Clam House, which was destroyed in the 1938 Hurricane. Dick Rogers remembers his father buying the land on which the new Fo'c's'le would be built:

What happened was he and George Thayer, together, bought from the end of the State Road down to the breakwater. George took the half closest to the state road and my father took the other half down where the docks were. But there was nothing there. So it didn't cost that much money. They wouldn't sell it hardly for any price before that because it was a money-producer for rent. But they couldn't do anything with it now without spending some money, so he bought it then in '38. Then they rebuilt it. I'd say it was going next summer. It might have been not full-tilt but there was not a big delay.

The new Fo'c's'le emerged from the ruins of the old. There can be no over-rating the significance of the Fo'c's'le in the history of Sakonnet Point. For nearly fifty years it served as the meeting place and watering hole for Sakonnet Point and indeed, for all Little Compton. One of the reasons for its success was its ability to attract and maintain a wide diversity of clientele. Fishermen, tourists, and summer residents all sat side-by-side at its long bar and enjoyed the views across the Sakonnet. If there were ever a place that could be described as a Sakonnet Point institution, it was the Fo'c's'le. Here is Bob Read on its importance:

Of course there are two iconic things that stand out in your mind when you think of Sakonnet Point. One is the Fo'c's'le, which was the dominant building on the Point and sort of the center of social life activity…The Fo'c's'le was a big center of activity and you could eat there, although I think you would want to be a little careful sometimes about some of the things that they served like their fritters were pretty heavy, but anyway, it was good. And then on Saturday nights, if you went down there, which we did occasionally, anybody and everybody was there. There were summer people, there were townspeople. It was a big center of social activity, and dancing going on, and you would all join in a big common dance that somebody would run. I don't think it was square dancing, but it was organized dancing. So that was a place where you'd get some good laughs anyway.

Fred Torphy agrees:

The Fo'c's'le was a great place. Again, it was a center of activity for summer people, for the fishermen, for people who just wandered in for dinner. It was a wonderful fixture at the Point. The bar in the evening was the center of a lot of activity. There was always either a ping pong or pool table in there. People come in and have a drink—it was very social—and it kind of cut across social lines. I think it was a gathering place for pretty much everybody.

And Tack Eddy also describes the intersection of different types of people who would meet at the Fo'c's'le:

The Fo'c's'le was a great place—meeting of town and gown. As I said earlier my parents met there. I spent a lot of time there growing up…Mike Rogers, we used to tease him about the clam fritters and things like that. I think I saw somebody get knocked out once one night by being hit by one of them… Anyway one of the waitresses there was Nina Blades. That's the widow of Mr. Blades Sr., Roy Blades. She was there. She was an institution.

Nina Blades is mentioned again and again in the oral histories. She was legendary among her fellow workers and the Fo'c's'le clientele. Dick Rogers remembered the time that a patron tried to give her trouble:

Nina, I'll tell you how well she was liked. She was kind of our head waiter, if you want to call it. Because she had been there a long time and we had a lot of college kids working there and they respected Nina… They had a big party one night the stuff was coming out a little slow from the kitchen 'cause the place was jammed. And a customer gave Nina a bad time and Nina was almost in tears. And I was tending bar at the time, because we were shorthanded and then the waitress came in, "You got to go talk to that customer. He's just giving Nina a bad time and she's in tears." I'm like, 'I ain't got the time to go out there now.' So it wasn't long, and another waitress came in, "You really got to go talk to that guy and straighten him out or you're not going to have a waitress in the place—we're all walking out." That's how devoted to Nina they all were.

Fisherman's Ball judges. From L-R: Frank Cornell, Charles Christianson, Roy Blades and "Kid" Macomber. Photograph. September 1945. Courtesy of Walter Elwell.

The Fisherman's Ball, held on the first anniversary of the 1938 hurricane, became a tradition that drew crowds to the restaurant. The format of the ball stayed more or less unchanged for many years: guests dressed as fishermen arrived bearing fish as tickets. Dick Rogers remembers the ball's origins:

> *And the ones that really got that going were Cang (Carrington) Lloyd—I don't know if you've heard of him and Pinky (Herbert) Brownell…Yeah, Cang Lloyd and Pinky Brownell. He had the rose garden. They got that started and they really were the ones who got it going down at the Fo'c's'le and that's when you bring a fish and they say you're going to put it in the chowder. Well of course it never got in the chowder. But it made for a good story and you know people would get up and tell fish stories. It was easy 'cause they told those kind of whoppers all the time. But like everything else it died out but that was really popular. The place was jammed. And Life Magazine, covered it, Life Goes to a Party. I can remember that clearly.*

Traditional music, dancing, and the telling of tall tales were all aspects of the ball, with prizes given for the best efforts in each category. Newspapers relished the opportunity to report on the event. The Third Annual Fisherman's Ball, held on September 24, 1941, drew exceptional notice from local newspapers. "Costumed in boots, overalls, and slickers," reported the *Fall River Herald*, "the fishermen, natives, members of the Summer Colony and visitors danced quadrilles and swapped fish stories to their hearts' content."[71] Mrs. Virginia Lloyd, dressed as a fishwife, sold fish at the front entrance to those who appeared without a ticket. It was a performance she would repeat often in future years.

The second Fo'c's'le was destroyed in the 1944 hurricane. The storm blew it from the ocean side of Bluff Head Road to the harbor side. And there it was rebuilt. The balls resumed quickly. At the Seventh Ball, held in 1945, Warren Blades won the award for the best fish story, telling a tale of some Gloucester fishermen who, 700 miles off the Grand Banks, tossed a penny overboard for luck. Two weeks later, according to Blades, the fishermen retrieved their penny while hauling their lead.

Doug Cory remembers these parties:

The admission to the Fisherman's Ball was a fish. There was a prize for the biggest one and a prize for the smallest one. I can remember being there one night when they had the Fisherman's Ball, I believe it was, and they started the bunny hop, and the building got going the same as the bunny hop. People jump and the building was doing this. They stopped it, naturally, because the whole thing was going to fall down. That's when Mike Rogers owned it.

The remains of the Fo'c's'le following the 1944 Hurricane. Photograph. Courtesy of Barrett Jennings.

Although the original Fisherman's Balls only survived into the 1960s, the Fo'c's'le itself would endure for another quarter of a century. Characters like Nina Blades and Marion Lima live on in people's memories. Then there is Andrea Phillips' story about the dog in the cistern:

Under the Fo'c's'le, for their drinking water, they had a big cistern. And Bud stored some of his fishing equipment down there and he went in to get it one day. He looked in the cistern and there's this Saint Bernard, this dead Saint Bernard, floating around in the cistern. It could have been a beagle, I don't know. And it could have been swimming. Anyway, but you know, the dog got bigger and bigger and deader and deader every year. And Bud apparently went up and said "Well if you're going be drinkin' the water, huh-u-huh, you better watch out for the hair, huh-u-huh." That was the one Fo'c's'le story that Bud just roared about every time he told it. It took on a life of its own.

In 1987 Dick Rogers sold the Fo'c's'le ending almost 50 years as a family business. Others continued to run the Fo'c's'le until 1991 when it finally closed its doors. Here is Dick Rogers musing on the end of the restaurant:

The biggest factor that made the business die out was air-conditioning... Well in the heat wave, we had weeknights that the Fo'c's'le would be full. And they would take a ride down there and you get that breeze and it wasn't only that but that was a big factor...Then they got the malls and they were air-conditioned. So you could go to the mall, why drive down here. And of course then they got air conditioning for the house. Then one summer the state tore up Sakonnet Point Road. It was bumpy, dusty and slow. It was devastating. It was the only summer I remember when we didn't make any money—that's how bad it was. And then in the next year it never came back to where it was...They didn't go looking for someplace else before. They were happy to come there, but when they couldn't, that was the end of that.

Fisherman's Ball

Tony Philippi, Oral History 2011 – The old Fisherman's Balls were fantastic. Anyone and everyone showed up. You had a band. You had dancing. I think you had food earlier but I was out fishing that night before I came in. For the largest bass there was a prize. *The Fall River Herald* was there photographing the whole thing. It was a great ceremony. You had a cup with the names on it; where that is I don't know. It was a wonderful, wonderful time, as I say, open to everyone.

One night that night a few years back Nate [Atwater] and I were out fishing. We had the bass cornered at East Island but they were all seven and eight pounders and it was almost pitch black. Bud Phillips came by with Nanny Wilder. And we said 'Hey we're going in. Why don't you catch some fish here?' But he said "No. They were going to Warren's Point; bigger fish." So they went off to Warren's Point. We went in, cleaned the fish, got them all ready and then we went to the Fisherman's Ball.

Well, at Warren's Point Nanny caught a 43 pounder and as soon as that fish was in the boat they gunned it back to the Fo'c's'le. And here comes Nanny with the fish still dripping; photographs: click, click, click; and she won it with a 43 pounder. Here's this great gal holding up this big fish. She had it stuffed.

Nanny Wilder. Photograph. Courtesy of Walter Elwell.

One time they didn't have any big fish but I had caught a 54 pounder a year or two before and had it stuffed. So we needed something. So I went home and brought the stuffed fish in, about this big, and I got my name on the cup too. We had something for the show. That was the Fisherman's Ball. Everyone was having a ball, literally; dancing, band, drinks, dinner; whatever you want.

World War II

The Original Little Old Lady – During the war I belonged to a large group of folks. We were college age mainly. Some went into the armed forces and the rest summered here. We rode out the '40s, partying and playing games. Our favorite hangout was the Fo'c's'le. We danced and did we ever sing!...and consumed lots of 'Narries' (Narragansett beers). We were riotous, rowdy and full of fun and stayed until we were thrown out the door.

A group of teenagers sang in the choir during 'The War' at St. Andrew's Episcopal Church on Sakonnet Point, big enough to seat 100 people. Sometimes on Sunday mornings, the Little Old Lady came home with the milkman. It was a project to switch her Fo'c's'le suit to the appropriate attire for church. 'Course folks had each had a pack of 'weeds' and numerous things to drink, like 'Narries' with their Saturday night dates. In the church the scent in the vicinity of where the choir was seated was pretty ripe. Louise Havens pumped the old organ, the squeaks and groans of which one could probably hear down at the Yacht Club.

Dick Rogers – In the '38 hurricane, my father bought the place and he had a wicked big mortgage. He didn't start out with a lot of dough. The army came down here to build a fort and they had soldiers here. Well the business down the Point helped 'cause there were a lot of people working there. The soldiers would come down to the bar in the Fo'c's'le and when that happened they had the Fo'c's'le open year round. At that time beer wasn't rationed but hard to get. We did so much business there that they came down with the delivery from the brewery with a trailer truck and my father had to quit using the bowling alleys 'cause he used that to store the beer. The mortgage was paid off way ahead on that one. Not that the war was a happy thing, but it livened up Sakonnet.

Caleb Woodhouse – This was the wartime in 1943 and there was a big coast artillery emplacement down across the pond where the Haffenreffer complex now is. Every so often a six-inch cannon would be wheeled out of the concrete bunkers. Occasionally they would have firing artillery drills, about which we were well warned beforehand, so we could get all the glass objects off the window ledges so that they wouldn't be shaken down by the report of the cannon. It was a drill. They wanted to have everything ready for any possible invasion, which decreased as time went on. But still those cannon reports made a dreadful noise and the house shook and our little dog Timber just went into hiding.

$3000 A SHOT

One of the fast-firing 6-inch guns at a Rhode Island harbor defense installation. At left, the entrance to ammunition chamber and power plant.

The Providence Sunday Journal clipping. April 21, 1946. Courtesy of David Haffenreffer.

Carlton Brownell – Oh yeah the Massey's Coach. Oh gosh yes. That stopped all the way along here. I have a snapshot of 1940 sometime when I was on leave from the army and my sister and a friend of hers were waiting for me right out here to get off the bus.

Caleb Woodhouse – Since it was wartime and there was rationing of gasoline, there was minimal driving around town, but also of meat, so we had to subsist, I smile as I think about it now, on fresh mackerel, caught that very day down by the harbor that the fishermen used to bring in. So we had fish again and again. But one day, along the beach we found a 5 lb. tin of salt beef from a torpedoed tanker off the coast. We brought it home and what a welcome relief that salt beef was, creamed up and served on toast, a nice variety from all that unwelcome fish.

The Stores

Lydia Brayton at the Bluff Head.
Photograph courtesy of Barrett Jennings.

Bob Read – There were two stores there. They were on the west side of the road—this is back in the '50s, I guess, and even '60s—Elsie's was a delicatessen there and they served ice cream and sandwiches. And there was another store. Somebody by the name of Brayton may have been running it. They sold newspapers and sneakers. We used to take our kids up there and buy sneakers.

Carole Davoll Flores – There were three stores; the Bluff Head which was Lydia Brayton, there was the Cove Market which was Elsie Johnson and then there was McCormicks. McCormicks was like a gift shop and an ice cream place. Lydia's was like that; the Bluff Head was like that and then of course, the Cove Market was a market; food and groceries. We used to go down to the Cove Market and get candy but I really don't remember my mother buying actual groceries there. I think mostly the summer people bought from Elsie.

Barrett Jennings – Lydia Brayton used to take care of all of the kids. That's where we would go. It was comic books and ice cream in the store. We had a bet that I would never get married. It was a five-dollar bet and she won. I loved Lydia.

Charley Soares – Elsie's. That was the only place I ever went in. I mean you went in and bought a package of devil dogs. That was my treat, a bottle of Pepsi—when I didn't have enough money at the Fo'c's'le to get a hamburger and have Nina Blades make me a nice big salad. It was funny sitting at the counter—there would be three or four other guys there and I would go in and if it was Nina or Mary or someone that I knew I would order French fries. They would have a plate of French fries like that heaping. The guy would say, "Well." I would say, 'It's a double order. I had to pay extra for the double order.' And the salad all nicely hand cut. But I remember when I used to go around the back and sell fish to Mike. Mike Rogers treated me well.

Shaw's Wharf. Detail from postcard. c. 1910. LCHS Collection.

Sakonnet Yacht Club

The Sakonnet Yacht Club was merely a year old at the time of the 1938 Hurricane. The club was established at its present location in 1937 by Howard Huntoon and Edward 'Tebby' Brayton, who purchased the crumbling Shaw's Wharf, incorporated as a non-profit and began selling shares. Randy Byers remembers the dock before the corporation bought it:

And the other thing I remember was just before 1938, where the present Sakonnet Yacht Club dock is now was an old dock and I mean old—it was rotten to the point where parts of it were down in the water and you could wade through and get to another part of it. And people had boats tied up to it at that point and in 1937—late 1937 to early 1938 it was taken away and the present dock was put up there. And that's about the earliest recollections I have about Sakonnet Point.

And Rod Perkins recalls the solid construction that went into the new dock:

During the summer of 1938 the corporation organized by Huntoon, Brayton and others caused a new dock to be built, in place of the remains of Shaw's Wharf. The construction was clearly first-rate, because the new dock survived the September 1938 Hurricane. The float went up the Sakonnet River in the hurricane, but apparently did not do any serious damage to the new dock as it swept away.

Rod Perkins also remembers the thrill of racing from the new Yacht Club on his sixteen-and-a-half foot sloop, *Curlew* in a Labor Day 'all boats' race:

I suspect that some 15 or 20 boats turned out for the occasion with the largest probably being Alex Royce's schooner "Discovery" or perhaps Harvey O'Connor's schooner "Volya," and with the smallest probably being a Herreshoff 12 ½. It blew hard from the southwest, and my brother Paul skippered the "Curlew" magnificently, with a crew consisting of myself and two others. The course was a leeward-windward course, around Old Bull bell buoy and back to the Harbor. To my delight our "Curlew" managed to come in third!

Perkins also explains the design of the Club's flag or burgee, which was undertaken at the time of its founding by club member Robert Foote:

Holding the burgee with its point facing downward, he said that the vertical blue line represents the Sakonnet River…The shorter, horizontal blue stripe, running east and west, represents Rhode Island Sound…With the point of the burgee still pointing south, Bob Foote said that the upper right quadrant of the burgee represents the land mass including Little Compton –the land east of the Sakonnet River and bounded on the south by Rhode Island Sound. The goose head in the upper–right quadrant had already been featured, I believe, in many Sakonnet signs and symbols, but Bob Foote adopted it with the explanation, which others can say whether it is true or false, that the word 'Sakonnet' in Indian language meant 'Home of the Wild Goose.'

Children at Sakonnet Point learned to swim off the Yacht Club's dock, whether they were members or not.

I suppose pure, unreflecting childhood happiness would be swimming in the harbor off the Yacht Club float and dock where I had—a big quantity of—a big lung capacity. I could stay underwater for about a minute at a time, sort of prowling along the bed. One time, somebody had—a sailor, a man had lost his eyeglasses off his boat which was at a mooring in the harbor and I guess he had heard that I was pretty good underwater with just holding my breath and going down and looking around. I found his glasses.

Caleb Woodhouse, Oral History 2010

The float was there. It was deep water so you have a chance to be thrown in or otherwise fend for yourself…And on Friday nights, inevitably, he would take me down to the harbor. We would go swimming at the Yacht Club…My father would take me down, as a little boy, and we would go for a dip—he called it. And what else can I tell you? We did a lot of crabbing there, with a gal named Sarah Wilder. Her nickname was 'Spook.' She was one of my best buddies growing up and we would go underneath the Yacht Club and catch green crabs and red crabs which we would then sell to Edna's Boat Service.

Tack Eddy, Oral History, 2010

When we were kids, because we lived at Sakonnet Point, we could swim off the Yacht Club. That was sort of an unwritten rule if you lived down there. I can't say we were always welcome there but we went anyway because it was our right of way or something. A few times we were asked to leave but we still went there. I don't think it's so much like that now. I don't think anybody would say you can't go on the Yacht Club but then again I don't know.

Carole Davoll Flores, Oral History, 2011

Although the float survived the 1938 Hurricane, Hurricane Carol in 1954 proved much more damaging to the Yacht Club.

I was on duty August 31 and opened up the clubhouse as usual. Since Hurricane Carol was expected to hit Sakonnet that day, the weather was deteriorating to the point that Howard Merriman, the Club Commodore, told me to open the floor hatches and leave. I went back to the 'big house,' our home on the harbor, and watched as the wind and waves increased. I remember seeing the Morrissey's shack floating through the harbor and cutting mooring lines of the few boats still anchored there. I also saw a small bass boat, I think it was the "Piscicide," being lifted up by a wave, crashing down on the rocks in front of our house and splintering apart. Shortly thereafter, I saw the Yacht Club steaming out of the harbor and up the river, a sad sight to be sure.

After the hurricane passed, I went back to the Yacht Club location to find only the pilings left. The Cove Market had been lifted off its foundation and was lying across Sakonnet Point Road.

Wayne French, Written History, 2011

The Sakonnet Yacht Club is now nearly three quarters of a century old. It remains an important institution at the Point, with its small building designed by local modernist architect Thomas Marvell. In the summer it is a hive of activity, with new generations carrying on the traditions of their grandparents (and great-grandparents) who had the foresight to establish the club.

Mrs. Hawes, Hat Hawes (Savage), Betsy Brayton (Dawson), Bunny Philippi (Millikin) at the Sakonnet Yacht Club.
Photograph courtesy of Bunny Millikin.

Sakonnet Yacht Club

Rod Perkins – Racing on Long Pond [pre-dates the Yacht Club and] was probably at its height in the years 1935, 1936 and 1937. At its largest the fleet consisted of probably 8 or 9 boats. My older brother, Paul, and I had a 12' flat-bottom skiff, with a single Marconi mainsail, named *Rowdy*. It was very slow. Josh Richmond had a 14' flat-bottom boat with a jib, and David Tappan had a newer boat (perhaps V-bottom), with a jib, which was named *Flash*. The queen of the fleet, and the fastest boat, was a lapstrake, round-bottom Dyer-built sailing dinghy, with varnished hull. Her name was *Flying Cloud*, and she was owned by Bud (Abbott) Phillips.

Howard Huntoon, 1987 – We bought the wharf rights and what was left of the property. The dock and the building were all that we bought. It was pretty dilapidated. The building on the inshore end wasn't all that bad, it was perfectly adequate, and it would have been a wonderful space. It was very open and roomy. It was just like a barn—it had two big barn doors on the front, and on the west side, at the end, there was a water tank. The Earl Hines family lived there in the upstairs.

In addition to losing the building (in the 1938 hurricane), the inshore one, a little child, one of the Hines children, was lost in that storm. It took that building out, see—the whole building went down—and of course Earl Hines' store was right next to it...The new dock fared better...although it seems just unbelievable. I think it cost the Yacht Club only about eighty-two dollars to take care of it, to get the dock straightened up again. Not the building. The dock was brand new. There were a whole lot of nets, trap nets that had come in all over the side. I remember it was an awful mess. But other than that, they just spiked some of the decking that lifted up. Of course, the float went up the river, and why the hurricane didn't take the end of the dock out, I don't know. I think it probably would have gone up the river if the dock hadn't been brand new. The float went up the river—it went upside down on Fogland. We got it back. It went up river again in the 1954 hurricane. It's the same one. I think the price on that float was three hundred dollars.

Bob Read – We never owned a boat ourselves but our children took lessons at the Yacht Club and so we would go out to that and I remember, before I was married, probably back in the late '30s or early '40s, I was invited to crew on a boat that John Alden was skippering and then in a race. Now John Alden, who was really the designer of the Alden class of boats that are sailed at the Yacht Club even today. He was the premier technician, artist, competitor. Everybody raced for second place when he was in the race. There was no question. He was a legend and I was privileged to be able to crew with him. I knew the rudimentary parts of sailing but he was the one that told me what to do of course. We won naturally, but that was an experience. Whenever his name comes up I am able to talk about that.

Hilary Woodhouse – Dr. Billy offered me a deal as an eight, nine year old, and that was to give him a hand. Giving him a hand initially meant that I would get down there on race day and I would pump the boat and I would rig the sail and then I would get his skiff and bring it around to the float so that everything was ready when he came down and then he and I would row out and he would, of course, skipper. He was so fair-minded he did not want to be aggressive in sailing. Now that's something that I found very difficult to live with because I was out to win and damn the consequences, so to speak. The thing that you had to remember is that Dr. Billy was also deaf, or extremely hard of hearing. He had hearing aids but they didn't work or he turned them off anyway. So when we were sailing in tight formation somewhere he was apt to give you instructions, but do so in such a loud voice that everybody all around you heard. "Okay we are coming about now." And of course everybody would know what your tactic of the moment was. I always thought that was a little unfair, a disadvantage to us. Plus, even though the rules of the road are quite clear in sailing, rights of way or such, he didn't put any stock in that. His only rule was you get out of the way of anybody. So regardless of whether you had the right of way or not, that didn't make any difference.

Noel Field – My second year as Commodore, there used to be a little Summer Association. Used to meet in the fall, have a party at the Golf Club. And in the Spring, people would get up from each of the organizations, and give this spiel about what was going to go on during the summer. Well we had just started with Sunfish, and I got up, in fear and trepidation as Commodore of the Yacht Club, and said we were gonna do something new this year, we were gonna require that all kids out on the water wear life jackets. And I didn't know what kind of reaction people—prior to that, the Aldens—nobody had ever tipped one over. Literally, you couldn't capsize one. And so the attitude of all the kids has always been, "Oh you wear a lifejacket, 'cause you can't swim!" So I get up in fear and trepidation and tell the assembled group—'We're gonna require lifejackets on all the kids, at all times, on the water.' And I got a standing ovation!

Phyllis Field – The Junior Program brought a lot of young people. Noel used to teach kids how to sail. There were always people who would teach kids, but it wasn't a formal program. But then we hired Dito Staley, who got the kids so excited about sailing, and we had Ruth Morton, and Chris Hornick, Janie Hutchins. All came as instructors. They were the first ones working under Dito. But more than anything else, he just had this power with the kids. So that was a great advantage to our program. Then, as the program became stronger, there was pretty active rivalry between the Golf Club kids and the Yacht Club kids. Although both, sort of, went to both clubs.

The Perkins Brothers on *Curlew* during Saturday races at the Yacht Club. Photograph by Blackmer Humphrey, 1940. LCHS Collection.

1954 Hurricane

***Jeanne M.*, *Audrey* and *Wild Goose* beached by Hurricane Edna. Edna hit Sakonnet two weeks after Carol.** Photograph courtesy of Barrett Jennings.

Barrett Jennings – So now, in 1954 I am ten years of age and we were summering every summer at the Point and you didn't have as much technology to let people know that a severe storm was coming. The storm came and it was hurricane Carol. Our cottage took in five feet of water. My great-grandmother lived with us and at the time of this particular storm. I went out with her to take her up to the *House on the Hill*, there isn't a *House on the Hill* anymore, but the Davoll's lived there at the time. I got maybe thirty feet outside the door and the wind was blowing. You know that something was going to happen. Two fishermen came out of nowhere and they helped my grandmother go up to the house. They took her up because the wind was so, so strong. I have never seen wind, to this day, as strong as it was.

Jim Mataronas – I was five years old when Hurricane Carol came on August 31, 1954 and my family didn't leave the Point. When the hurricane got so it was almost on us, my father decided to leave and we couldn't leave because Round Pond had flooded so that the water was going over the road. It was about two feet deep. So we went up Montana Road around by Gus Bounakes' house. He was a lobsterman. We had to go up there to higher ground. We got to the corner at the Stone House and stayed in the barn where, at that time, Wilcox's fishing nets were stored. We sat on the nets that were piled high with the door open and watched the hurricane. Then, while we were waiting and watching, all of the rats and wildlife were coming in looking for a place to hide because the water was so high. We stayed there for a couple of hours.

Barrett Jennings – I only know the house as Winslow. They were very nice. In the '55 hurricane that's where we stayed. So we stayed at Davoll's in the '54 and in the '55 hurricane we stayed at Winslow's house. What I really remember, is boulders going just down the road, which would be Rhode Island Avenue. Still, to this day, I can see them and I couldn't believe how big they were, just rolling down. It was like the 4th of July with the poles—the electricity. Ron Mackay and I went across the road and we got Mrs. Campbell, who was Dr. Lloyd's secretary. We helped her come over to Winslow's house.

James Waite – I was one of the only people allowed down at Sakonnet Point after the [1954] hurricane. My dad was scalloping out of New Bedford. I went down to see Carl Wilcox and he used to try to get ahold of the boat my dad was on, and to this day I'm not sure which one it was. It was either the *Red Star* or the *Bright Star,* and anyhow, one of them went down all hands on deck. I used to go down every morning and Carl would try to get him on the shore radio. We never did get ahold of them. My mother was real nervous. So anyhow, it was probably a week after the hurricane. My dad called up from Virginia and he said, "Hello. I want to send you some money. We didn't have too good of a trip so we are going to go back out again." She says, "Okay Lewie." Well that was the last time my father went out the door. She said, "That's it Lewie. You are not leaving me with five kids again."

James Bounakes – After the storm subsided the next day we walked up the beach and there was just nothing but rubble. Houses and everything were just smashed to pieces there. There was looting going on too. People would come from out of town. They were stealing outboard motors, bass fishing reels, all kinds of fishing gear and things like that. My father's boat stayed there in the hurricane and he had huge anchors on it. It had three, 500 pound anchors.

Saving the Nasuluga

Holder Wilcox on the *Nasuluga*. Photograph. c. 1955. Courtesy of Douglas and Susan Cory.

Douglas Cory, Oral History 2010 – Holder Wilcox had a fish company, H.N. Wilcox Fish Company. I went to work for him in the early '50s. He had six or seven traps and it was a pretty good system. He had a small boat, the *Nasuluga*, which was named for the granddaughters, the first two initials of each granddaughter. Nahma, Lucinda, Susan and Gail. I managed to stay with him for twelve years or so, I guess, before I went on to other things. They were excellent people. And in the course of it, I rode out the 1954 hurricane with Carl (Wilcox) on the *Nasuluga*.

It was a day that the wind was starting to blow a little bit when we were at Sakonnet Point in the morning. We actually planned to go out and pull the traps. We sat in the building for awhile and Captain Wilcox says, "I don't think we are going to do much here today." So we sat there playing cards and the tide started to rise and it got up so that the boats were coming up onto the pier and fish boxes were blowing around. So Carl said, "I'm going to take the boat away from the dock. One guy comes with me." He said, "Doug, you come with me." We went and got on the *Nasuluga* and went over by the Yacht Club and anchored.

First we tried to pick off people from two boats—two people and two kids actually that were on a small sloop and two people on a small yawl in the harbor. It was so bad then and the wind was probably 70, 75 miles an hour that we couldn't get near them because we were beating them up more. Later on both boats went aground up to Taylor's Lane.

They survived, but there was a man named Jan Telenga. He raised turkeys on the land back of the Old Bull, just the next point up from Taylor's Lane. Well he had turkeys and he had guard dogs. When the boat went aground the people got off all right but one of the children was bitten by one of the dogs quite seriously. Then he got into bumblebees that had been stirred up by the storm and the bumblebees bit the other kid pretty badly. I guess they both recovered.

We let another man go off of his mooring and he went up to Seapowet on the way going to Stone Bridge and the boat tipped over. It was 43, 44 feet long. That was the *Wanderer*, but it tipped over, end over end over end. It was so rough and it was bad here.

We went and anchored in the corner. We had two 500 pound trap anchors and a 100 and a 175 pound anchor. We were right over next to the Yacht Club and water kept rising. There were buildings on the Point. There was Mack's Store. He had all kinds of things in there. He had charts and gear for fishermen and so forth and it had a double building. There was a big building on the east side with a flat piece in between. Carl says, "What's that? Look. Watch the next wave." So one of them came and hit the back of the building and it broke out that little piece in the front. The next one came and took everything. The whole building went demolished. Flew into many pieces.

In the meantime, the tide was still rising and there was a man who was anchored in the harbor with a Steelcraft boat. It was maybe 30 feet long. He had two people with him, a woman and a child. Well, they finally got the anchor up, got the engine running, because there was so much stuff in the water, it got up into the engines and plugged the sea suctions up. He got them free and he got the boat started and he went over the sea wall, underneath the telephone wires, all the way up the road where Mataronas lives now, right through the pond, all the way to back of the Stone House, when he ran aground. He dropped his anchor. They all got off and went up the road. The boat was there for six months or a year after that because he said he didn't want anything to do with it. He said that was it.

While we were anchored in the harbor, Carl said, "Go up on the bow and slack off on the port anchor a little bit," so it would make it ride a little easier. Well, I went around the corner of the wheelhouse and here something goes past in the air. Carl says, "What the hell was that?" I said, 'A chicken.' He says, "A chicken!?" I said, 'Yes.' So when I tell people I have seen a chicken doing a hundred and ten miles an hour they think I'm crazy. But what had happened was Dr. Lloyd had chickens in a coop down on the end, towards the lighthouse, and the water got up high enough so that it broke open the chicken house and the wind—it was clocked at a hundred and ten—would pick these chickens up, because they weren't flying but all of a sudden you would see a chicken go by.

We rode out the storm and when the eye came along everything just calmed right down and we had a chance to regroup and tie off our anchors a little better. We had to take the sea suctions apart down below and poke the strainer off the end so that the water could get back into the engine. Carl kept it running for awhile and then, after the eye went by, the wind was blowing so bad it came right around from the other direction and everything that was left in the harbor went onto the beach with the exception of Cang Lloyd's. His was the only one that was left and the rest of them were on the beach, but we got two of the anchors up and we went back to the dock. Everything was gone. The buildings were all gone, the dock was all gone. Holder and the rest of the gang went up to Davoll's and stayed there during the storm. After the storm died down, they came back and helped us get tied up the best we could. At least we saved the boat.

Finding the Malolo

Reg Howe, Written Memory 2011 – Hurricane Carol struck Tuesday, August 31, 1954 in the morning. We had just sat down in the living room to watch events outside when Matt [Hawes] appeared at the head of the driveway. He had come to ask me to go back to his grandmother's house to stand on the sea wall and watch the surf. At that point my mother intervened, absolutely prohibiting either of us from going anywhere. Soon, as the storm surge arrived, we could see great brown clouds of earth erupting over the Austins' house at the foot of Old Bull Lane. In the strongest gusts our plate glass picture window bowed in about three inches, and for whatever good it might have done in the event of a rupture, we pulled the curtains.

Carol moved through quickly, and by late morning the worst of the storm had passed. Matt and I were freed from house arrest to go out and explore. Considerable wreckage lay in the Ham's field, including our rowboat and the Yacht Club's float. Most if not all the houses on the shore side of Taylor's Lane South had suffered water damage, some quite serious. The power lines were down. The sea wall in front of Matt's house rested in pieces; the high water mark had reached close to the front steps. A large schooner which had left the harbor to seek shelter up the river had foundered off Old Bull and washed up at the foot of Taylor's Lane.

After taking in the immediate sights, Matt and I decided to hike along the shore from Taylor's Lane to the harbor. While the surf remained spectacular with waves still cresting the lighthouse, the sun had started to poke out. In our journey, we came across hardly any people but the shattered remains of most of the boats in the harbor, including the Hawes' Alden, *Malolo*. She had come ashore not too far from Bailey's Ledge. The stern had separated from the rest of the hull, and we decided to carry it home as a souvenir. It was an arduous trek, roughly three miles over a rocky and wreckage strewn beach. Even by itself the stern was quite heavy, and at age 13 we were scarcely musclemen.

Lobstering

Charley Soares – There used to be a lot of territorial disputes. One of the boys used to go out in the fog. He used to have ten lobster pots, but whenever it was foggy, he'd have a hundred. He'd come back with more lobster than you ever saw, and I think it was Gus who went to Warren's Point and waited for the kid to come by and let a couple shots go from the 06 [shotgun] from Warren's and that kind of killed the enthusiasm. I remember that day. I remember George Davoll and a couple of the old timers laughing about it because they said, "Well that will teach that person not to be snickering lobsters like that."

John Gomez – When they had a cafeteria at the school you could buy something or bring your own lunch. And someone from a lobstering family, he'd have lobster sandwiches, and that's about the only thing. He'd eaten so much lobster he'd swap a lobster sandwich for grape jelly. They'd choke on lobsters. People can't believe that today, now.

Jim Mataronas – I started lobstering in 1963. My license was five bucks. I was thirteen years old. Lobsters were 45¢ a lb. I went lobstering before I went to school. I bought a pickup truck when I was sixteen and drove to school. One morning I got to school (J. F. Wilbur school on the Commons was grade, middle and high school those days) and I was kind of late so I was still wearing my boots and all and my work clothes and was going to change. Before I could get through the door, I was written up. So the next day I wore my boots into school! After that they never bothered me because they knew I wasn't out to smoke—they realized that I was going out and working.

Fo'c's'le waitress Eleanor Carroll poses with lobster pots. Photograph. 1969. Courtesy of Walter Elwell.

Fishing in the Post-War Years

Despite the destruction wrought by Hurricane Carol, which finished off most of the commercial structures at Sakonnet Point, fishing continued to be viable, although in different ways from the past. Caleb Woodhouse associates his earliest memories of Sakonnet Point with the smell of fish:

Modern day trap fishing. Photograph. Courtesy of Donald Gomez.

> *I could just smell this very strong odor of fish. Where did it come from? Well the fishermen of the "Nasuluga" dried their nets out in the meadow and then, once they were dried, the seaweed fell off and the gulls swooped in to pick off the remnants of dead fish. The fishermen would mend the nets. The nets were always out there and if we wanted to cut across the fields on the way to walking down to the shore or the beach we tripped over the nets at first and then we learned to raise our feet and not do it. Anyway, that's where we lived a rather simple life. The presence of the fishermen—the fish, the nets, the fishermen and the people—was very much a part of it.*

And some of Carlton Brownell's earliest memories are of going to the Point for fish:

The crew of the *Nasuluga* mending their nets. Photograph. 1955. Courtesy of Douglas and Susan Cory.

Well I think the first thing I remember is going down with my father to either buy lobsters or fish because when the boats came in you could buy them right then and there…Right ahead of it was called Bluff Head Market. And that was a fish market. And I remember they dumped all the offal—right over the side of it—right near the breakwater. Not much sanitation, or worry about it.

One of the great characters of Sakonnet Point in the mid-twentieth century was Holder Wilcox, proprietor of the H.N. Wilcox Fish Company. Wilcox was known for his boat *Nasuluga*, named after the first two initials of each of his four granddaughters (Nahma, Susan, Lucinda and Gail). Wilcox was wiped out in each of the three hurricanes, but always returned with a sense of humor and a kindness to children that is still remembered. Doug Cory worked for Wilcox and married his granddaughter Susan. Doug remembers:

In the spring of the year they depended on scup and squid. That was their main—what they caught—and then later on it went to fluke and sea bass and everything was shipped through a local fish dealer, Parascondolo, and was shipped to New York to go to the fish market. So, and then in the wintertime, the boat, naturally, when there was no fishing, they went dragging for shellfish up the bay—Sakonnet River.

Tack Eddy mentioned the different types of fishing at the Point, and how the industry evolved as different stocks began to dwindle.

You have lobstering. You have inshore lobstering, and then probably in the late '60s, early '70s, a man named Macomber from Westport and others started going offshore. And that's just opened up a whole new area to lobstering. But most of the people like Jimmy Blades and the Mataronases and others originally had their pots in close. So that was one fishery. At one point—you have always had the trap boats down there, as long as I have been living.

Tack Eddy also enjoyed fishing, practical jokes, and combining the two. Here he describes a novel use for unwanted fish:

I would set my trap in there, catch some minnows, 'borrow' somebody's boat. Sometimes it was the Yacht Club skiff, somebody who wasn't looking, whatever. I would take it and I would go out to the mouth of the harbor and, with a hand line, I would catch flounder for dinner. We also did a lot of spear fishing. We would go to Old Bull. We'd go to Sheep's Pen. We would go out to the islands. We would go off the leader line at the second tee. Mainly we shot tautog, but sometimes stripers. We would get a lot of tautog, come back and quite often we would end up heading home and dumping tautog in people's mailboxes as we went home.

Holder Wilcox. Photograph. c. 1955. Courtesy of Douglas and Susan Cory.

All sorts of oddities came up in the nets. Jim Mataronas remembers an uncomfortable encounter with a shark:

I can remember working on the dock and there was a shark that went by that was twenty feet long. It seemed to look right at me with that big eye and kind of turn on its side as if to get a better look at me! I was standing on the dock, Brayton and Manchester's dock—there used to be three trap companies. An old fellow named Crow Gray—lived on Neck Road at Four Corners, Tiverton—and the shark went by and he was long so they didn't want to put any straps—because it wasn't Tony Parascandolo in those days—it was Holder Wilcox and Carl Wilcox—was the son, Carl. So anyway, they decided they were going to go harpoon it. So they got in the boat and it was swimming around the harbor because there was bait and stuff and it smelled good—in the spring. I always remember—I looked down and he turned up

Clark Snow on the Sakonnet dock. Photograph by E. Atwater Byers. 1984.

at me and he looked right at me—I will always remember that softball sized eye and his head was like two feet wide and twenty feet long. So they went out with a harpoon and harpooned it. And then they got a 'Nantucket sleighride'—which is when the fish takes off after you have speared him! I thought this guy has got to be crazy. All the fish has to do is turn around and jump in that boat and sink the whole thing. So it towed him for about a hundred feet and the harpoon pulled out and we never saw him again.

The era of trapfishing, in decline for a century, began to hit bottom in the late 1960s and early 1970s. Fred Torphy began to notice the decline at that time.

Although the fishing, I would say during those times, I remember as a kid that the trap boats would come in every day with a ton of fish, all different kinds of fish. They were running full blast and I think slowly but surely I noticed during the—probably the '70s, maybe starting with the '70s—it became a lot more difficult than it is now to sustain a fishing operation because the amount of fish. I think it was the numbers of boats increased and it affected the Point as it did New Bedford.

And swordfishing, which was briefly a staple of the Point, went into a tailspin at the same time. But despite the dwindling stocks and the controversies over regulation of fishing, the industry continues at the Point as it has for hundreds of years. More than the resorts, hotels, restaurants and other businesses, the harbor, which was first called 'Fishing Place Cove,' has sustained the lives of generations of fishermen, their families, and the people they feed on a daily basis. It remains the one constant in the history of the Point.

Swordfishing at Sakonnet

Fred Torphy, Oral History 2011 – The harpooning of swordfish probably went out in the '70s. It changed to long lining, which they do much further out. But when I grew up, the Bounakes and the Blades families were a part of the swordfishing fleet. Jean Bounakes would have a marine radio. If there was word that the boat had a swordfish, I would go down with my parents and we'd wait for the boat. We'd see what they had gotten. These were big fish. Sometimes 300-350 lbs., almost 400 lbs.

They would hoist them up on the dock and go through this ritual of chopping off the swordfish's head. If you were really lucky, you might be able to get the sword. The kids prized those. Then the fish would be taken to the market right on the Point so that the next few days, if anybody wanted it, they'd have wonderful, fresh swordfish.

These were beautifully designed swordfish boats with crows' nests on top. They would travel at a very slow speed and try to find a sunning swordfish. If they did see one, then the person from the crows' nest would signal and the boat would slowly creep up on the swordfish and then someone would get out onto the swordfish stand with a harpoon. You had to be very, very good at it. The harpooner would have to have a sense of how the fish was moving and he would try to strike the swordfish.

Then the swordfish would sound. It would go down and the rope would play out which was attached to the harpoon. Then at the end of it would be a red keg and the keg would disappear as well. It was like the old whaling method. Then they would wait for the keg to come up which would mean the swordfish had tired and they would bring it in either by skiff, or they would pull on the line, and finally get the swordfish in.

I remember Roy Blades told me once that he was with Gus Bounakes and he had gotten as far as getting the keg in the skiff and they were pulling the swordfish in and the line went slack. They thought they had lost the swordfish and then all of a sudden the sword came right through the bottom of the skiff. Roy was just sitting on the keg in the skiff and the keg came up, hit him in the chin and knocked a tooth out. It was a swordfish that turned against him.

David Brayton on the pulpit. Photograph. LCHS Collection.

Swordfishing

Joan Burhendorf – A bunch of them had these sports fishing boats, Cang Lloyd, Gus Bounakes. If they were flying their yellow flag, that meant they had a swordfish. And we would get dressed and run down to the Point because they would weigh the fish and clean it right there on the docks and people would take bets on how much it weighed. And then you had Earl Hines from the Cove Market or Mike Rogers bidding on it, to buy it to sell, or in Mike's case, serve it at the Fo'c's'le. So that was another big deal.

James Waite – Well UWB was one of Dave Brayton's nephews. He got the nickname UWB because he would be up in the mast with Dad [Lewie Waite] and he would look at the swordfish and stuff. And Ben is looking way out like that. My father would say, "Well there is a swordfish right there." And Ben would say, "Where Lewie? Where Lewie?" And he would say, "Underwater Ben." It stuck, UWB, Underwater Ben.

Tony Philippi – There were about nine boats. The primary boat of this group was David Brayton in the *Xiphias*. And then Don Austin would go out, but he was working running a truck depot or something. He would go out in the *Dolphin* which was just a beautiful boat. There was Tebby Brayton and *The Wahoo*. Tebby Brayton would be on board in his three piece thick wool suit and the spectacles. On the weekends, Nolan Greer would go out on *The Nomad*. He has Basil Davoll going out on the *Claire* but not when I was going out. You had Tom Haire with the *Andiamo* which was a 36 foot Brownell where David's was a 32 footer. Gilbert Manchester took the rig off his trap boat; he would go out on the *Islander*. And then you had Steve Peresteros, the Greek restaurant owner and he would try and get a crew for the *Poppy* and he would be out there. And Bud Phillips would go out in *Surfmaster*. He was the rod and reeler. And Nanny Wilder was his main customer for trying to catch a swordfish on rod and reel, which is probably the most difficult fish in the world to catch on rod and reel.

Bud Phillips and Nanny Wilder with the crew of *The Surfmaster*.
Photograph. Courtesy of Andrea Phillips.

Sakonnet Light. Photograph by Mike Steers. 2010.

Sakonnet Point. Photograph by Mike Steers. 2010.

A Fragile Balance

What is Sakonnet Point today? How does it differ from the world of the Sakonnet tribe, the Lyman Hotel, and even of Holder Wilcox just fifty years ago?

Although the hotels and bathhouses and fishing shacks are gone, the sense of place that has developed over the last four centuries survives. Much of the Point remains open and relatively undeveloped. The houses that line the quiet lanes are modest and small, and generally built in a seaside style that developed more than a century ago. Fishing boats, pleasure craft, and visitors to Lloyd's Beach all evoke the sense of continuity on the Point and help define it as a popular refuge from the cares of the world.

But not everyone can always agree on what is best for the Point. In recent decades, contentious debates have taken place concerning its future. One of the earliest of these was the controversy over expanding the breakwater in the mid-1970s. The improvements, first proposed by the Town Council in 1975, included a 500-foot length expansion of breakwater, the dredging of a wider, deeper channel through the harbor, and construction of a wharf large enough to accommodate much larger offshore fishing vessels. The plan,which neatly divided the town into partisans and opponents, was extraordinarily controversial. Proponents argued that the extension and associated improvements would make the harbor more accessible to more large fishing boats, thus leading to the possibility of more offshore fishing and therefore new job opportunities. Opponents argued that the impact on the environment would be severe, and that the potential for accelerated industrial and residential development would be significant. By a vote of 356 for and 414 against, the breakwater expansion was defeated at the largest Financial Town Meeting on record.

Construction of the private Sakonnet Point Club, on the approximate footprint of the Fo'c's'le, also did not go without comment. Some saw the replacement of the Fo'c's'le, arguably the most significant long-standing public space in the Point's history, with a private club as an affront to the Point's traditional open nature. Others argued that the presence of the club revived activity at the Point and was, at the very least, a use that was compatible with the area's maritime history.

The extensive renovation of the Stone House, including its successful nomination to the National Register of Historic Places, has been the most recent change at Sakonnet Point. The restored hotel and the establishment of upscale dining is a revival of the Point's long tradition of hospitality and a challenging business to run in a changing economy.

What is clear is that Sakonnet Point remains a special, almost magical place for many different people: fishermen, bird watchers, sailors, year-round and summer residents, and for anyone who simply enjoys walking on the beach. Although the visible reminders of Sakonnet Point's past are few, the natural beauty of seemingly endless horizon continues to define the place. People interviewed for this project attested to the Point's timeless value. Above all, their memories of the characters who made the Point what it is live on. Here is Susan Cory remembering the people of Sakonnet Point:

> *People would come from all over. You would see such an incredible mix of people on the dock. I don't mean big crowds, but you would see wealthy people. You would see fish dealers. It would be the guys that were working there. It would be the girls that might be hanging around. It would be people asking Grandpa, "Mr. Holder, Mr. Wilcox, will you clean this fish for me please?" And nine times out of ten, he'd clean it.*

Sakonnet Point and its legacies of natural beauty and historical change endure. This sentiment of endurance is captured perfectly by Caleb Woodhouse:

That's the beautiful thing about the place. There is, despite some of the superficial changes—architectural changes, there is this timeless beauty that you smell, that you see, that you look across the pond at the sunset, looking over St. George's tower on Newport, the ocean, the way the rocks become bare at low tide, the sand, the birds, everything. It is, really, endlessly beautiful.

The last word here belongs to our adventuresome Mariana Tallman, whom we have quoted several times throughout these pages. Her description of Sakonnet in 1894 holds true today, and speaks again to the 'timeless beauty' of the place:

Did ever any one sail to Sakonnet and come home disappointed? Breathes there a man with soul so dead who ever to himself hath said, "I don't like Sakonnet?" Quiet little corner that it is, it has all the grandeur and beauty of the wild Maine coast, the breeziness and freshness of the wind-swept meadows, the strength of the hills and the majesty of the sea. Unspoiled… it offers sweet wild freedom and rest to the seeker.

Could we ask anything more of a place?

Photograph. Late 19th century. LCHS Collection.

The Preservation of Sakonnet Harbor, 1975 to 1985

Karl Haffenreffer, Former Chairman of Harbor Watch, Written History 2011 – In 1975 the Town Council requested that the Corps of Engineers plan a development project in Sakonnet Harbor. Congress granted the request. The Corps planned to build a 500' (initially a 950') northerly breakwater, dredge a wider, deeper channel, erect a dike off the barrier beach 10' higher than the shore's grade, dump dredge spoils behind it, and pave the fill to make a quay for 65-70' offshore fishing boats, some over the tidal-exchange culvert into the wildlife refuge. Since the Town was liable for any costs exceeding the $2 million federal limit, the Council promised to obtain Town Meeting approval before signing a contract. Support was widespread, but a few people conditioned their support on the resolution of certain problems. Then, on January 5, 1981, the Planning Board voted unanimously that the "ill conceived" project would "upset the traditional balance" of uses in the harbor and jeopardize the Town's finances and adjacent residential property values. I submitted to the 1981 Annual Financial Town Meeting a stroke approving the Project, but urged its defeat. 108 voted for the Project, 183 against it. The Council disregarded the vote because it had not submitted the stroke.

Harbor Watch was organized in September 1981 by over 250 inhabitants opposed to the project's environmental and financial impacts. In late 1981 the Chairman of the Harbor Advisory Board urged that a private developer be allowed to drive sheetpiling as far as he liked across the Town-owned barrier beach and make a quay of it. On March 18, 1982, the Council requested that DEM downgrade the harbor's water quality from SA to SAm, a new classification that permitted new or expanded marinas in the cleanest waters. Harbor Watch led a statewide campaign to have DEM expunge SAm. On May 10th 300± people—the State's largest environmental hearing as of then—adjourned from an overflowing Council Chamber to the gym. Opposition to SAm was overwhelming.

It was the lead story on three channels. In its wake DEM expunged SAm. Two nights later came the Special Town Meeting called by the Council to approve the project. Letters to the editor, full-page ads, mailings and canvassing produced the largest Town Meeting that anyone could recall. 356 ballots were cast for the project, 414 against it. The Council respected the vote. The Corps deauthorized the project.

Breakwater. Postcard. c. 1965. LCHS Collection.

A coastal geologist retained by Harbor Watch pronounced Sakonnet Harbor Beach a barrier beach. In July 1982 Harbor Watch quietly persuaded the Department of the Interior to include the beach in the Coastal Barrier Resources System, which bans federal funding for development. The designation withstood a dogged counterattack: Interior received more comments on this beach than on all the beaches in Texas. Harbor Watch convinced the CRMC to lower the water use category along most of the harbor beach from Type 5 (high intensity) to Type 2 (low intensity). Harbor Watch led a statewide campaign that persuaded the CRMC to change 17 "Developed" (hence highly developable) barrier beaches, including Sakonnet Harbor Beach, to "Moderately Developed," a new category that bans intense development.

The Point Today

Bob Read – You know I can't regret what has happened really. I think change is inevitable and you have got to bend with the change. You have got to live with it. Maybe you have got to resist it when there are certain basic principles of integrity—that you have got to fight against certain changes. I think what has happened there, it has been a community effort basically, trying to clean up the Point with the storms and the hurricanes and the lack of money to do anything otherwise. I think, in retrospect, if I had my druthers—and it's hard to second guess what has happened—but I would like to have a park up there. I kind of wish that the Town had been able to convince the citizens to vote to spend the money to clean up the Point and make it into a park and make it accessible to anybody and everybody down there to visit and fish.

Mike Steers – It is surprisingly the same as it has always been, an incredibly beautiful part of the world. Not frozen in time but evolving with time, allowed to move forward as a working viable community, while preserving so much, the islands, Seaconnet Point Farm (without the animals), the lighthouse, the harbor, the yacht club, swimming off the dock and rocks, the commercial fishing, the trap fishing, the marina. It is all still there with generation after generation in the same houses expanded for family and friends, holding dear all the treasured memories and making new ones. It is still a summer colony with just a few year-rounders. Exploding with activity at the close of school in June and quietly closing down from Labor Day through Thanksgiving for the long winter's nap.

Photograph by E. Atwater Byers.

Endnotes

1 Colonel Benjamin Church, Diary of King Philip's War, 1675-1676, quoted in "Awashonks, Sachem of the Sakonnets" by Dora Atwater Millikin in Portraits in Time: Three Centuries of Remarkable Residents, 1600-1900 (Little Compton, RI: Little Compton Historical Society, 2008), 15.

2 Benjamin Franklin Wilbour, Notes on Little Compton, edited by C.C. Brownell (Providence, RI: College Hill Press, 1970).

3 Janet Lisle, The History of Little Compton: First Light: Sakonnet (Little Compton, RI: Little Compton Historical Society, 2010), 136-137.

4 Wilbour, quoted in Lisle, 136.

5 Little Compton Land Evidence [LCLE] (Little Compton Town Hall), Volume 3: 490-491.

6 LCLE Volume 3: 633.

7 LCLE Volume 3: 633.

8 LCLE Volume 3: 634.

9 Francis E. Sargeant and Robert R. Bottin, Jr., Case Histories of Corps Breakwater and Jetty Structures, (Vicksburg, MI: United States Army Corps of Engineers, Waterways Experiment Station, 1989), 74.

10 Baird, Spencer F., Report of the Condition of the Sea Fisheries of Southern New England, (Washington, DC: United States Government Printing Office, 1871), 200.

11 Baird, 203.

12 Mariana M. Tallman, Pleasant Places in New England and How to Reach Them, (Providence, RI: The Providence Journal Company, 1894), 96.

13 Tallman, 98.

14 Tallman, 98-99.

15 Sheila Higgins, "A Tribute to "Elsie" (undated clipping, possibly from the Providence Journal), Little Compton Historical Society (LCHS) scrapbooks.

16 Nicholas B. Wainwright, "The West Island Club," Newport History, Vol. 50, Part 2 (Spring 1977), 22.

17 Wainwright, 21-22.

18 Wainwright, 23-24.

19 Tallman, 95.

20 Carl Haffenreffer, "Sakonnet Lighthouse" (Sakonnet Scuttlebutt, July 1969), 3.

21 Anonymous, "A Night in Sakonnet Point Light" (Providence Journal, 7 November 1886), LCHS Scrapbook.

22 Anonymous, "A Night in Sakonnet Point Light."

23 Haffenreffer, 3.

24 Haffenreffer, 4.

25 Tallman, 96.

26 Anonymous, "If You Were Assigned to Sakonnet, You Could Only Hope You Had a Compatible Partner or Else...," Sakonnet Times, 23-24 March 1988, 3.

27 Anonymous, "Aged Couple Saves Drowning Man's Life," Pawtucket Times, 6 January 1911.

28 William H. Durfee, "Lighthouse Keeper Recollects September Hurricane of 1938," Sakonnet Times, 1977, 5.

29 Haffenreffer, 4.

30 Faith Wilbur, "Friends Breathe New Life into Battered Sakonnet Lighthouse," Sakonnet Times, August 7-8, 1985.

31 Sarah H. Whitman, "Seaconnet Point, R.I.: Nightfall on the Seaconnet Shore." In Poems of Places, edited by Henry Wadsworth Longfellow (Boston and New York: The Riverside Press for Houghton Mifflin Company), 242-243.

32 Bayles, Richard M., History of Newport County (New York: L.E. Preston & Co., 1888), 1038.

33 Donald T. Gomez, "Colonel Henry Tillinghast, 1831-1910: A Little Compton Swashbuckler," in Portraits in Time: Three Centuries of Remarkable Residents, 1600-1900 (Little Compton, RI: Little Compton Historical Society, 2008), 84-85.

34 Bayles, 1038.

35 Robert Grieve, The England Coast: its Famous Resorts, (Providence, RI; J.A. & R.A. Reid, 1891), 41.

36 Gomez, 85.

37 Henry D. Lloyd, "Story of the Building of the Watch House," typescript on file at the LCHS.

38 "For Rent, Furnished," undated brochure, LCHS Collections.

39 George McDonald, "Era in Little Compton Ending," undated Providence Journal article, LCHS Collections.

40 McDonald, "Era in Little Compton Ending."

41 Rhode Island Historical Preservation Commission, Historic and Architectural Resources of Little Compton, Rhode Island (Providence, 1990), 25.

42 Wilbour, 251, cited in Rhode Island Historic Preservation Commission, 24.

43 Wilbour, 251.

44 Wilbour, 97.

45 Wilbour, 253.

46 Bayles, 1027.

47 Grieve, 41.

48 Springfield Republican, 19 June 1900.

49 Tallman, 92-93.

50 LCLE Volume 20: 46.

51 Pawtucket Times, 26 June 1915.

52 Springfield Republican, 27 July 1919.

53 LCLE Volume 23: 342.

54 LCLE Volume 25: 349.

55 Lloyd Family Letter (writer and addressee not clear) given by Jessie Lloyd O'Connor to LCHS. Letter is dated "Sakonnet R.I., 25 June 1906."

56 Martha F. Patten, "A Reminiscence of Sakonnet," in Wilbour, 280-281.

57 Frank E. Sargent, The New England Coast: its Famous Resorts (Fall River, MA: Frank E. Sargent nd), 104.

58 Tallman, 92.

59 David Patten, "H.B. Cook was Purser of Queen City," Providence Journal, undated clipping in LCHS scrapbook

60 David Patten, "H.B. Cook was Purser of Queen City," Providence Journal, undated clipping in LCHS scrapbook.

61 David Patten, "He Saw Steamboat Queen City's Great Tragedy," Providence Journal, 2 April 1956, clipping in LCHS Scrapbook.

62 David Patten, "He Saw Steamboat Queen City's Great Tragedy," Providence Journal, 2 April 1956, clipping in LCHS Scrapbook.

63 Broadside, LCHS collections.

64 David Patten, "Before the Auto Ruined S'cunnet's Steamboat Business," undated Providence Journal article, LCHS scrapbook.

65 Pawtucket Times, 8 July 1909.

66 Wilbour, 240.

67 "Little Compton Recaptures Heroism of Hurricane," undated Providence Journal clipping, LCHS Scrapbook.

68 "Sakonnet Point Fisherman Relates Thrilling Experience," undated Providence Journal clipping, LCHS Scrapbook.

69 "23 Families Lost Homes in Sakonnet Point Area," undated Providence Journal clipping, LCHS Scrapbook.

70 Clipping from Fall River Herald dated only 1939, LCHS Collections.

71 Fall River Herald, 25 September 1941.